CONTENTS

INTRODUCTION

Quilts don't always have to go on beds and they don't have to be huge for us to enjoy them. In fact, there are many benefits to making a little quilt: they don't require a huge investment of fabric or time, they require very little space for laying out and making, they are great for trying out new techniques and skills, and they can be basted together on a table top and then quilted easily, whether by hand or machine.

For many people, using pre-cut Jelly Rolls™ is an economical and easy way to venture into the world of quilt-making. Jelly Rolls™ lend themselves wonderfully to little quilts as the size of the pieces is ideal for a small quilt. Of course, you can cut strips to size yourself, especially if you don't want to use all your Jelly Roll™ collection at once – this will allow you to eke out the loveliness, using a bit here and a bit there. Personally, I like to save every piece of leftover fabric, and use odd scraps of Jelly Rolls™ in my little quilts so that every last piece of a collection that I have loved can be put to good use.

Little quilts are an ideal way to continue our quilting tradition. There is a well-documented history of little quilts, used both as doll quilts and as crib quilts, so it is not a new concept to make little quilts to be used in our homes or shared with others. If we look back at quilts from the past, the fabric pieces were small, and the quilts were too. Some of the quilts in this book were inspired by those old ones, and the sizing here was made easier due to the pre-cut size of the Jelly Rolls™. Many of the old quilts were made from scraps from the scrap basket, and again we can do that today. Even if we don't sew all of our own clothes, many of us often have much-loved scrap fabrics left over that can see their way into a quilt.

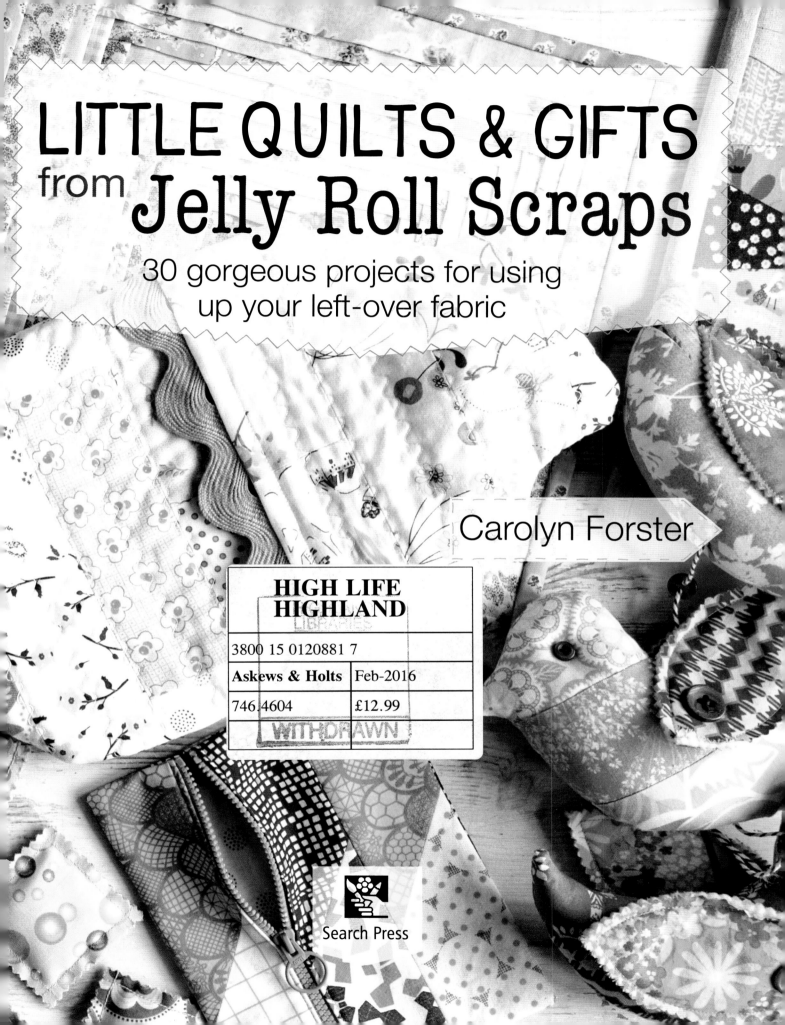

LITTLE QUILTS & GIFTS
from Jelly Roll Scraps

30 gorgeous projects for using up your left-over fabric

Carolyn Forster

Search Press

ACKNOWLEDGEMENTS

Thanks to the team at Search Press for allowing me to indulge in endless days of stitching and then making it all into such an amazing book. Thank you to Becky Shackleton for having such a great vision as to how this book would look and making it all happen.

Thanks to Craig and Paul for putting up with it all.

Thank you to all of my students who continue to inspire me with their enthusiasm and quilts.

First published in 2015

Search Press Limited
Wellwood, North Farm Road,
Tunbridge Wells, Kent TN2 3DR

Reprinted 2015

Text copyright © Carolyn Forster 2015
Illustrations by Jane Smith
Photographs by Fiona Murray, pp. 1–7, 12–13, 30–71, 74–121
Photographs by Paul Bricknell, pp. 8–11, 14–29, 72–73
Photographs, illustrations and design copyright © Search Press Ltd 2015

ISBN: 978 1 78221 006 1

The Publishers and author can accept no responsibility for any consequences arising from the information, advice or instructions given in this publication.

Readers are permitted to reproduce any of the items/patterns in this book for their personal use, or for the purposes of selling for charity, free of charge and without the prior permission of the Publishers. Any use of the items/patterns for commercial purposes is not permitted without the prior permission of the Publishers.

Suppliers
For details of suppliers, please visit the Search Press website: www.searchpress.com.

Some of the Jelly Rolls™ used in this book may no longer be available. Look for something similar or cut fabrics from your stash. Fabric collections come and go very quickly, as do Jelly Rolls™. It is always worth buying a Jelly Roll™ when you find one that inspires you and keeping it until the right project comes along.

Printed in China

Publisher's note
All the step-by-step photographs in this book feature the author, Carolyn Forster. No models have been used.

If you don't want to hang your little quilts or use them as crib or doll quilts, you could always transform them into other practical items, such as table mats or pillows. Use the basic pillow-making method on pages 102–105 and you can convert quilts to pillows in no time.

Or if you fancy turning your hand to a few other techniques, continue the fun with your leftover Jelly Roll™ scraps and stitch some gorgeous gifts and keepsakes. There is a wide range to choose from, from the quick and addictive lavender ravioli (pages 100–101) to the covered folder (pages 86–89), which takes an afternoon, but is well worth the time spent. From the toy octopus (pages 90–93) to the tablet case (pages 120–123), there is something for everyone, and for every occasion too. I will introduce you to an old style of patchwork here, in the form of the Manx Log Cabin, used as a decoratively textured table mat (pages 74–77), and continue with hexagons that require no setting in of seams, with the use of the half-hexagon template (pages 102–105).

Use some of the projects as a starting point and then make them your own. Choose colours and fabrics to suit the recipient in mind. Play around with the basic ideas. For example, the hanging birds look great with a branch of rosemary secured underneath each body, as they look like they each have their own branch to sit on, and they smell nice too. Some of the projects are machine quilted, but if you have some time to spend, then do hand quilt them if you'd rather. Use straight lines either in big-stitch or fine hand quilting and you will see a different quilted texture emerge. Whichever project you choose to work on, enjoy the process, and be happy knowing you are using every last scrap of your favourite Jelly Roll™.

MATERIALS

WHAT IS A JELLY ROLL™?

A Jelly Roll™ is a pre-cut fabric roll of 40 strips of fabric, cut 2½in (6.5cm) wide. They are cut across the width of the fabric and are approximately 44in (112cm) long. The name 'Jelly Roll' is trademarked to Moda Fabrics, but other fabric manufacturers also supply similar products as a precursor to their own collections of fabrics too, but under different names. Make sure you check the width of the strips before you start any of the projects, to avoid disappointments. Buying Jelly Rolls™ makes the piecing and cutting processes fast and easy. But bear in mind that there is nothing to stop you cutting your own Jelly Roll™-sized pieces of fabric. The instructions for cutting your own strips are provided on page 14.

As they are all from the same collection, the fabrics in a Jelly Roll™ will all work well together. But it can be fun and satisfying to make a project your own by working in a few new fabrics. When choosing additional fabrics, make sure they are a similar weight to your other fabrics so as not to cause undue strain on the seams and so that there are no extra considerations when laundering.

BACKING FABRICS

The backing fabric you choose should be a similar weight to the Jelly Roll™ scraps and other fabrics used on the quilt top. This will make the piece easy to work with if you decide to hand quilt it. However, it is worth considering that if you are machine quilting you can get away with a slightly heavier-weight fabric, as the machine will be doing the hard work for you.

The great thing about working on little quilts is that you may already have enough backing fabric to hand, as the quilts will often need only a three-foot square (square-metre) piece of fabric or smaller. You will need to ensure that your backing fabric is larger all round than your quilt top, to accommodate the shrinkage or 'pulling up' that occurs as you quilt. You will later trim off this surplus fabric when you bind your quilt.

WADDING (BATTING)

Wadding (also known as batting) is the soft layer of filling that you will place between the patchwork top and the backing fabric. For little quilts I tend to use a wadding (batting) without too much puffiness, or 'loft': I usually find that this looks better in proportion to the size of the quilt. I tend to prefer 100% cotton wadding (batting) with scrim, although there are many other alternatives available.

For these little quilts you may find that you have enough wadding (batting) already to hand. However, I always think that small projects are a good excuse to experiment with different types of wadding (batting), to see how they feel and how they look in the finished quilt. Many shops sell trial sizes of wadding (batting) or will cut 20in (half a metre) widths, so the financial investment is not too great.

THREADS

It is worth investing in specialist threads for the different stages of your projects. I usually choose a pure cotton sewing thread for sewing my quilts and gifts. Use a colour that merges well with your fabrics: my frequently used colours are cream, dark cream, tan and grey. When stitching appliqué though it is best to use thread that is the same colour or a shade darker than the fabric you are appliquéing down.

Specialist tacking (basting) thread is ideal for hand tacking: it is easily broken and is cheaper than regular sewing thread.

Quilting thread is slightly thicker than general sewing thread as it needs to hold the three layers of your quilt together. The reels that you buy will state whether they are for hand or machine quilting (or both). For fine hand quilting use a 30 or 40 weight thread by your favourite manufacturer. Try out different makes as they all have slightly different properties and come in different colours. Try out different types to see the results before you use them on your projects. For big-stitch quilting a thicker thread is best, such as cotton perlé (or pearl cotton). The best weights are numbers 8 or 12. All these threads will come in variegated as well as solid colours, and it is worth trying out the variegated to see the subtle difference it can make to your quilting. Again, I prefer to use 100% cotton threads where I can, but use your favourite.

TOOLS

HAND SEWING

Pins

Long, fine pins are good for keeping fabric and seams in place until you stitch. Remember to try to pin perpendicular to the seam and remove the pins before machining over them. For appliqué, smaller specialist appliqué pins are well worth the investment, as they allow you to stitch without you or your thread getting caught up in them.

Iron and ironing board

A good hot iron, with or without steam, will be useful at every stage of your work. Always press when indicated in the project instructions, making sure that the iron is hot. You can use steam when pressing seams if you like. Either have the ironing board set up close to where you work, or use a table-top board next to your machine if you don't want to be constantly getting up and down.

Hera marker or chalk wheel

These tools allow you to leave a non-permanent mark on your work when you want to mark for placement or for quilting designs. The chalk wheel will leave a line of powder that will easily brush away. The Hera marker will make a crease in the fabric that will disappear over time.

Quick unpick

No matter how careful we are when stitching there is always something to unpick at some stage. This tool will make life easier when that time comes.

Template plastic

This is a sturdy but thin plastic that can be drawn on or traced through and then cut with normal scissors. To write on the plastic, you should use a fine permanent marker pen.

Needles

Use needles from a quality manufacturer as these will make all the difference in your work. General sewing needles in a range of sizes will be fine for finishing off projects. For fine hand quilting use Betweens or quilting needles in sizes 10 or 11. They should pull your thread through smoothly without the need to tug. For big-stitch quilting use Betweens, quilting or embroidery needles size 6.

Thimble

Using a thimble as finger protection when sewing or quilting is often an acquired skill. It is worth getting used to some protection on your fingers, and there are lots of different variations on the market to try out. I use a round dimpled thimble on the middle finger of my right hand and and a flat-top ridged thimble on the index finger of my left hand.

MACHINE SEWING

A basic sewing machine with a straight stitch is all you really need to make the quilts and gifts in this book. Make sure you always work with a sharp needle that is replaced regularly for the best results. Check your machine often for a build up of fluff, and carefully clean it out to help it run smoothly.

If you choose to machine quilt, the addition of an even-feed (walking) foot will help. This foot is also useful when stitching layers of fabric and wadding (batting) together, such as when you add a binding. If you have a machine with a selection of decorative stitches then these can often be used for machine quilting in conjunction with your walking foot.

CUTTING

Scissors, large and small

Good sharp scissors are a worthwhile investment as they make accurately cutting fabrics easy. Keep older, duller bladed pairs for cutting wadding (batting) and card and paper. A small sharp pair will be best for threads and careful snipping.

Rotary cutter, cutting mat and rulers

These tools will help you accurately cut and measure your fabrics. However if you're mainly using pre-cut strips then you might not need to invest in all of them. See how you manage without and then when your budget allows, buy the set.

Specialist rulers

These rulers work with the rotary cutter and mat. You can use them as templates too, but all the templates for the shapes you need to cut are given in the book.

Template materials

Templates can be traced or photocopied and cut out and then stuck to card or template plastic. Thin card such as cereal boxes can be easily used, but for something more durable it is worth buying specialist template plastic sold in most patchwork shops. These more durable templates will remain in shape no matter how many times you use them.

Pencils for marking fabric

The best way to mark your fabric for cutting is with a propelling or retractable pencil. You can get these in sewing shops, often with different coloured leads, so they will always show up on the fabric. Make sure you angle the pencil in towards the template and cut along the drawn line for the most accurate results.

LITTLE QUILTS

TECHNIQUES
DESIGNING YOUR QUILT

A great advantage to making little quilts is that you do not need much room to lay them out and plan them. Often you can use space on a table near where you are stitching, or put a wide-width piece of felt or design-wall gridded fabric on to the bed or floor and you can plan and play on that. Your design can then be easily lifted up and moved. If you want to create a portable design wall, purchase an A2 sheet of light-weight dense foam board from a do-it-yourself or art supply store. Cover your board with wide-width felt or design-grid fabric. Smooth it on to the front of the board, and secure to the back with double-sided tape. This way the patches will stick to the board as you arrange them, or you can secure them more permanently with pins.

CUTTING YOUR OWN STRIPS

The easiest way to cut your own strips is with a rotary cutter, a cutting mat and a wide ruler. Using a gridded, transparent ruler makes it easy to see the width of the fabric you're cutting. Begin by washing, drying and ironing the fabric.

Note
These instructions assume that you are right-handed and work from left to right; if you are left-handed, work from right to left.

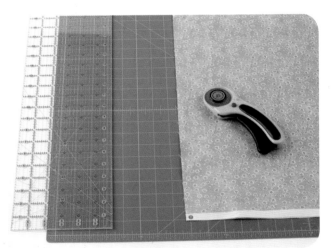

1   Fold your fabric in half with the wrong sides facing and the selvedges together. Lay it on the cutting mat so that the selvedges are at the bottom and aligned with a horizontal line on the grid.

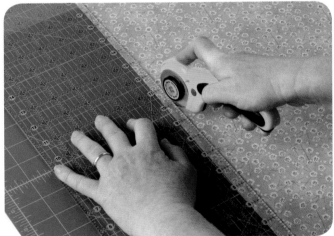

2   You will need to trim approximately ¾in (2cm) from the left-hand edge. Align the ruler with a vertical line on the grid and hold it securely in place. Keeping the cutter firmly against the ruler, push it away from you, starting at the selvedge.

3   Remove your trimmed fabric edge. Carefully align the ruler so that it lies 2½in (6.5cm) from the left-hand edge and cut again to create your first strip.

4   Place your cut fabric strip to one side. Repeat step 3 to create as many strips as you require.

CUTTING SQUARES AND RECTANGLES

1   Lay your 2½in (6.5cm) wide strip of fabric horizontally on the cutting mat, aligned with the background grid with the selvedge on the left-hand side. Trim off the selvedge and discard this.

2   Measure along with the ruler to where you want to cut – 2½in (6.5cm) for a square; the required distance for a rectangle. Align the ruler with the grid and cut. Remove the shape and continue to cut more in the same way, as you need them.

How many can I cut?

As a handy reference tool, I have listed below the number of shapes you can expect to cut from one 42in (106.5cm) strip:

+ Sixteen 2½in (6.5cm) squares

+ Nine 2½ x 4½in (6.5 x 11.5cm) rectangles

+ Four 2½ x 8½in (6.5 x 21.5cm) rectangles

+ Twenty-four half-square triangles

+ Twelve quarter-square triangles

CUTTING TRIANGLES

For triangles, because of the added complication of accommodating the seam allowance, it is easiest to use specialist rulers when cutting your fabrics. These rulers are available for cutting half-square triangles (squares that are cut into two triangles) or quarter-square triangles (squares that are cut into four triangles). Follow the manufacturer's instructions when using them, as they all vary slightly.

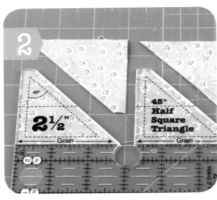

1   Place your fabric strip on the cutting mat and align it with the grid. Align the left-hand edge of your ruler with the left-hand edge of your fabric. Starting at the bottom, carefully cut away from yourself, along the edge of the ruler.

2   Continue to cut along the vertical and diagonal edges of the ruler to create your interlocking triangle shapes.

CUTTING DIAMONDS

Some companies have created templates that fit the 2½in (6.5cm) strips to help you to create shapes with the seam allowance already calculated. You can buy a variety of templates, including hexagons and coneheads, and here I will show you how to cut a diamond shape.

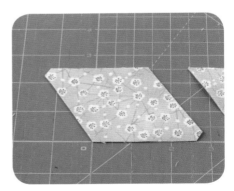

1   Lay your piece of fabric down on the cutting mat, aligning it with the background grid. Put your template in place, then push your ruler against it. Holding the ruler firmly in place, remove the template and cut along the ruler. Replace the template on top of your fabric.

2   Holding the template firmly in place, cut along the right-hand edge with your cutter.

3   Remove your template to reveal your cut shape. Repeat as many times as necessary.

USING TEMPLATES

Making templates from firm card is a good option, but a better one is to use template plastic as this will not wear out or change shape over time. Measure the template for sizing after you have copied or traced it to ensure accuracy.

1   Place your template on top of your fabric. Draw around it with a fine, sharp pencil: propelling pencils work well as they are always sharp. Angle the pencil in towards the template, not away from it, so as not to make the shape larger.

2   Remove the template and cut out along the drawn line, so as not to make the shape bigger or smaller. Check your fabric shapes against the accurate template.

Before you start to stitch...

Here is some useful guidance to help you before you start any of the projects in this book. Although it may be tempting to dive straight in, I would advise that you carefully read through all the instructions before you start a project. Make sure you have all the materials and equipment to hand, and that you are familiar with the techniques used.

Remember

+ all seam allowances are ¼in (5mm) unless otherwise stated
+ all fabric cut off the bolt is cut across the width, including your Jelly Roll™ strips if you are cutting these yourself (see page 14)
+ all fabric quantities are based on a 42in (106.5cm) useable width of fabric

Machine stitch length

Your stitches should be small enough to hold the fabrics together securely, but large enough to unpick easily, should you need to. Set your straight-stitch length to either 11 or 2.0 to 2.5, depending on your machine. However, when you sew strips together that will later be cut and re-sewn (such as in the Divided Nine-Patch Quilt, pages 36–37), you may want to set the length a little smaller than this so that the stitches do not come undone easily when cut.

Pressing

Press your work regularly with a hot iron; I press my work from the front. Take your time to position the work and the seam you want to press correctly so that you only need to iron it once.

CHAIN PIECING

This is a quick way to join pieces of fabric together in pairs, and will help you to reduce wasted thread. You will feed the paired pieces of fabric under the machine foot, one after another, continuously sewing but leaving a gap of about ½in (1cm) between them. The paired pieces of fabric are then held together by the line of thread, hence the term 'chain piecing'.

1   Arrange all your fabric pieces together in pairs, with right sides facing. Place the first pair under your machine foot and stitch the seam. When you reach the end, continue stitching for about ½in (1cm) to create a small 'chain' of stitches, then feed the next pair under the foot and continue until they are all joined.

2   Simply separate your fabric pairs by cutting the threads joining them together.

LAYERING AND BASTING (TACKING)

Once your patchwork top is complete you will need to layer it with wadding (batting) and your background fabric before you quilt it. Lay your backing fabric down face down, place your wadding on top, then place the quilt top on top, facing up.
   There are several methods you could use for basting (tacking) these little quilts. Aim to baste (tack) every 5in (13cm) or so: this might mean that you only need three or four lines of stitches in each direction.

Start with a backstitch and a knot and work the stitches from right to left (left to right if you are left handed). The stitches should be about ½in (1cm) long and evenly spaced. Finish with a backstitch to keep the thread secure. Use a long, strong needle and a tacking thread. Popular needle choices are Cotton Darners or Sharps size 8. When basting a quilt I find it easier to work to a standard grid system.

Alternative methods

Other options for basting (tacking) include safety pins, spray glues such as 505, and tacking guns. With all of these methods I would still recommend basting (tacking) around the outside edge of the quilt to stabilise it during the hand-quilting process.

APPLIQUÉ

Appliqué means 'to apply' – so for our purposes, stitching fabrics on top of each other.
Here I used an appliqué stitch and chose a thread that matched the fabric that
I was appliquéing down. Cut the thread as long as your arm to make stitching easy.
If you are using a template, freezer paper is ideal as the shiny side sticks to the
fabric when ironed, stabilising it while you work.

1 Cut your freezer-paper template and iron it, shiny side down, on to the wrong side of the fabric. Cut out the fabric, leaving a ¼in (5mm) seam allowance all round.

2 Turn the seam allowance over to the wrong side and tack it in place around the entire shape, working through the fabric and the template.

3 Pin the shape in place. Knot your thread then insert the needle from the back. Bring it through the edge of the fold of the appliqué shape and pull the thread through. Take the needle back down through the background fabric only, in the same position as it came up, making a tiny stitch over the edge of the appliqué shape.

4 Take the needle about ⅛in (0.25cm) along the back of the work and then bring it back through the folded edge of the fabric. Repeat steps 3 and 4, creating a row of tiny stitches on the front of the work. Work your way around the whole shape, but leave a 1in (2.5cm) gap. Leave the needle and thread attached. Remove the tacking stitches.

5 Push a flat tool between the paper template and the applique fabric, to separate them.

6 Pull out the paper template through the gap in the stitching. Stitch the opening closed.

7 To fasten off, work two or thee stitches on top of each other through the background fabric only in an area hidden behind the appliqué shape.

HAND QUILTING

Before you begin, make sure you know how to start and stop stitching securely. This sounds basic, but it will prevent you wasting time going back over stitches that have come undone.

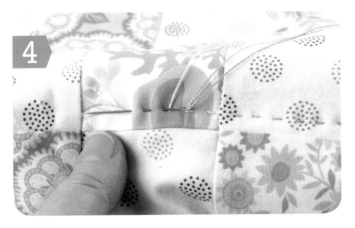

Starting to stitch

Cut a piece of thread about the length of your arm – this is a comfortable length to work with. Tie a knot in the end, then thread your needle.

1   Working from the top of your fabric, insert the needle though the top layer of fabric and batting, to the left of where your first stitch will be. Bring the point of the needle out where you want your first stitch to start.

2   Pull the thread firmly to embed the knot in the wadding (batting). The embedded thread will be quilted over, giving your stitching extra security.

Note

If the knot is difficult to pull through the fabric, use the needle's point carefully to expand the hole in the fabric that the knot needs to fit through. Once the knot goes into the wadding (batting), use your needle to push the fabric threads back into place.

3   Insert the needle to the right of your thread, to create your first stitch through all three layers of the quilt, then bring the needle out through your fabric to the left of your stitch.

4   Continue to stitch across through all three layers of the quilt creating a neat, even line of stitches.

Finishing off

When you come to finish off a line of stitching, make sure you leave about 5–6in (13–15cm) of thread.

1 Complete your last stitch then take the needle through to the back of the quilt. Bring it up at the start of the last stitch.

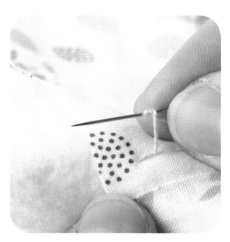

2 Wrap the thread around the needle three times, keeping it close to the quilt, as shown.

3 Insert the needle back through the fabric, into the wadding (batting), underneath the middle of the last stitch. Bring the needle up a short distance away. Pull the knot through gently to embed it in the wadding (batting). Snip the tail thread.

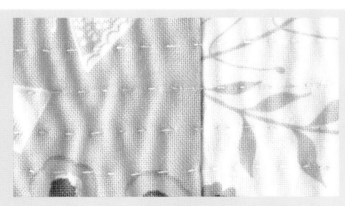

Little-stitch quilting

Little-stitch or fine hand quilting is a simple running stitch that creates a textured design. Choose a simple cotton thread to create this effect. Select a complementary or contrasting colour to match your design, and try to keep your stitches small and even.

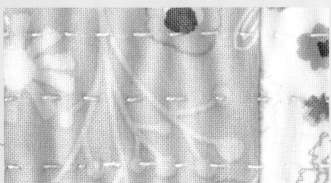

Big-stitch quilting

This quilting method uses a thicker thread and bigger stitches than little-stitch quilting. For this reason it quilts up faster and gives a bolder, more primitive feel. Choose a Chenille size 22 or 24, Betweens size 3 or 5, or a Sashiko needle. A cotton perlé size 8 or 12 is a good choice of thread.

MACHINE QUILTING

Fit your machine with a quilting or 'jeans' needle and use a specialist machine-quilting thread. Use the foot that you like best: I find that an even-feed (walking) foot works best as it helps the layers to work through at the same pace.

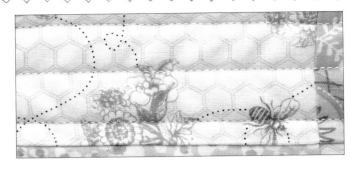

Quilting styles

Select the stitch type and length to suit the quilt you are working on: I have used both straight and wavy machine stitches on these little quilts, but you could always experiment with other types of stitching, or even with free machine embroidery using an open-toed darning foot.

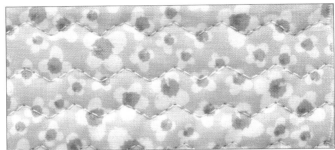

USING TEMPLATES FOR QUILTING

Amish wave

Over the years, many church groups have used this quilting design. For this reason, the basic fan-shaped design goes by various names, each associated with a particular group, such as the Amish wave, Mennonite fan, Baptist fan and simply Wave. Use the template given here, or scale it up and down to suit your quilt design.

Template arrangements

You can choose whether to quilt this fan-shaped design either from the outside edge of the quilt in towards the centre, or in rows from bottom to top.

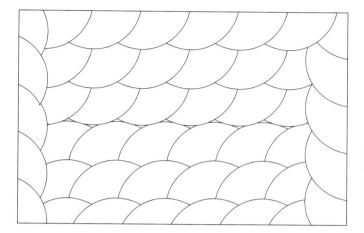

Amish wave worked from the outside in.

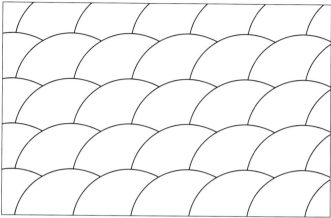

Amish wave worked in rows from the bottom to the top.

Using your template

1 Create your template using the guidance on page 17. If you are right-handed work from right to left; if you are left-handed work from left to right. Align the bottom of the template with the bottom of the quilt top and draw around the arc using a propelling fabric marking pencil for a clear thin line.

2 Move the template along, aligning the right-hand edge of the template with the arc you have just drawn. Draw in the second arc, then move the template again. Continue in this way along the bottom of the fabric then add in additional rows as necessary.

3 The arcs can then be quilted from top to bottom by hand. The inside lines can then be measured and marked with a dashed line or judged by eye. When each large arc is full move on to the next one. The distance between these inner arcs can be adjusted according to the size and design of your quilt, but you could consider using either the length of your needle or the width of your thumb knuckle as a guide.

BINDING

Here I will show you two ways to bind your quilt: the first method is done after quilting and requires you to cut or create strips long enough to bind each side of your quilt. The second method takes place before quilting, see pages 26–27.

JOINING STRIPS

I use a bias join for joining strips together, which means there is less bulk when the fabric is folded over and wrapped around the edge of the quilt.

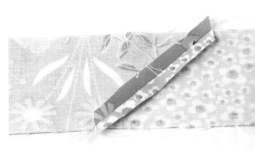

1. Take a fabric strip and lay a second fabric strip at 90° on top of it, right sides facing. Allow an extra ½in (1cm) of fabric along each short edge. Stitch across the diagonal.

2. Join subsequent strips as in step 1. Continue to add fabric strips until you have a piece that is long enough to go round all four edges of your quilt. Trim off the excess fabric leaving a ¼in (5mm) seam allowance.

3. Press the seams open to minimise the bulk.

FINISHING: SQUARE-CORNERED BINDING

This is a great binding for little quilts, as often less than a single Jelly Roll™ strip is needed for each side. You can easily use a different fabric on each side of the binding to add some quirkiness, or use two and have them on opposite or even adjacent sides. Play around with different ideas on each quilt and see which suits it best. You can even use up small pieces here too. I suggest that you use the bias join, as seen above, to minimise the bulk when the binding is turned over and give a neater finish.

1. Fold the binding in half lengthwise, wrong sides together and press. Sew to the side of the quilt, matching the raw edges and using the width of the presser foot as your seam allowance.

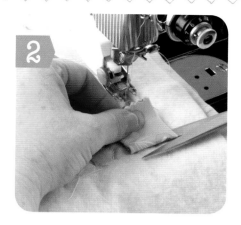

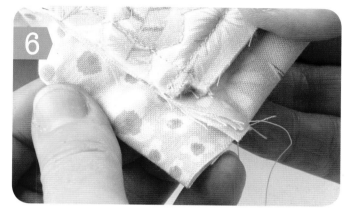

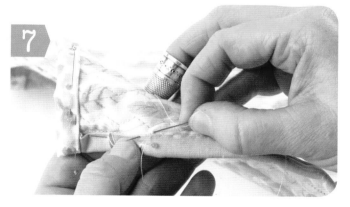

2 When you reach the end of the first side, trim off any excess binding so that it aligns with the top fabric. Repeat on the opposite side of the quilt.

3 Trim away the excess wadding (batting) and backing fabric along your two sewn edges. Trim to align with the raw edge of the binding.

4 Fold the two previously attached binding strips back then position the third strip of binding: aligning the raw edges.

5 Sew along the length of the binding and trim off the excess when you reach the end. Repeat on the final side.

6 Snip away a small square of fabric and wadding (batting) at each corner to help reduce the bulk.

7 Turn the binding to the wrong side of the quilt, folding it so that the raw edges are concealed at the corners and pin. Slipstitch the binding in place.

8 When you reach each corner, sew along the open edges of the fabric to secure them.

FINISHING: TURNING THROUGH

With this method, also known as 'Bagged Out' or 'Patch Pocket', the quilt is in effect bound before it is quilted! This method works well with little quilts when an added binding does not seem necessary. To hang the quilts with this finish either add a sleeve (see page 28) or hang with a skirt hanger or decorative curtain pole with rings with clips.

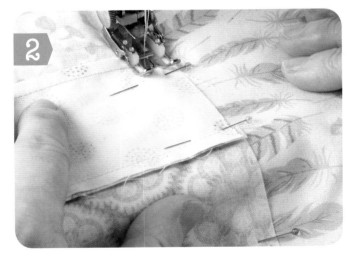

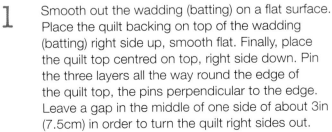

1   Smooth out the wadding (batting) on a flat surface. Place the quilt backing on top of the wadding (batting) right side up, smooth flat. Finally, place the quilt top centred on top, right side down. Pin the three layers all the way round the edge of the quilt top, the pins perpendicular to the edge. Leave a gap in the middle of one side of about 3in (7.5cm) in order to turn the quilt right sides out.

2   Stitch round the edge of the quilt top using a ¼in (5mm) seam allowance and the walking foot, removing the pins as you reach them.

3   As you come to a corner, stitch across it at an angle using two or three stitches, as this will help you get a neater corner when you turn the quilt through. Secure the stitches where you start and stop.

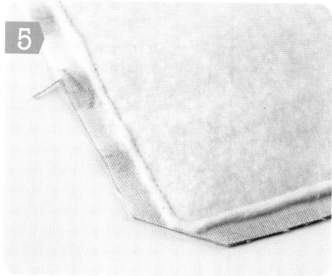

4   Trim the wadding (batting) and quilt back to leave a ¼in (5mm) seam allowance.

5   Snip across the corners through all three layers. Use a pair of small sharp scissors to trim the wadding (batting) close to the sewing line.

6   Turn the quilt right side out, poking the corners and 'rolling' the seam between your thumb and forefinger to help it lie flat. Slipstitch the opening closed.

7   Either pin or use hemming clips to keep the edge flat. To keep the edge in place permanently use one of the stitches below:

Big-stitch: sew along the outside edge of the quilt just along where the bulk of the seam allowance ends.

On the machine: use the walking foot and increase the length of the stitch so it is longer than for piecing. Secure the three layers together beforehand if you need to, using safety pins or a tacking gun.

DISPLAYING LITTLE QUILTS

The great thing about small quilts is that it is easy to find the wall space to display them. Either hang one individually or group a few together and you can perk up any room space in an instant. There are many ways that you can hang your quilts, but here are two that you might like to try.

Hanging sleeve

1   Cut a piece of fabric 4½in (11.5cm) wide, and as long as the width of your quilt, minus 1in (2.5cm). Turn a small ¼in (5mm) hem at each short end of the fabric and stitch this in place.

2   Fold the strip in half lengthways with the right sides together. Stitch the long edges together to make a tube or sleeve.

3   Turn the sleeve the right way out. Press it so that the seam is in the middle of one side.

4   Pin the sleeve in position, so that it is just below the binding and equidistant from the binding on each side of the quilt. Slip-stitch the sleeve in place along both long edges.

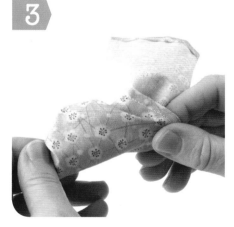

Hanging your quilt

To hang the quilt, cut a piece of 1 x ¼in (2.5cm x 5mm) flat wooden dowling to the width of the quilt, minus ¼in (5mm). At each end of this, on the thin edge, screw in the eye of a hook-and-eye set. Thread this through the sleeve. Attach the hooks to the wall, then hang your quilt up, hiding all your fittings.

Hanging corners

1. Cut two 4in (10cm) squares. Fold each one in half diagonally, wrong sides together and press.

2. Prepare the quilt for binding by trimming away the excess backing and wadding (batting). Line up each corner triangle with the raw edges aligned.

3. Pin in place and tack or stay stitch on the machine 1/8in (3mm) away from the raw edges to hold in place.

4. Bind the quilt as you would normally. See pages 24–25 for square-cornered binding.

Hanging your quilt

With the corner pockets in place, cut a length of round dowling about ½in (1cm) in diameter that is long enough to fit in the pockets and run across the top of the quilt. On the wall, nail in two picture hooks to hold the dowling and hang your quilt.

SPRING BRICK WALL QUILT

20½ x 20½in (52 x 52cm)

This little quilt made from simple
rectangles was inspired by brick walls
covered with climbing flowers and trailing
plants. I alternated one main fabric with
a selection of scraps, but use as many
or as few fabrics as you like.

YOU WILL NEED

BRICKS
Fifty rectangles, 2½ x 5in
(6.5 x 13cm): cut twenty-
five rectangles from a lightly
patterned floral fabric and twenty-
five rectangles from assorted
floral fabrics

BACKING
22 x 22in (56 x 56cm) square

WADDING (BATTING)
22 x 22in (56 x 56cm) square

BINDING
Four strips of 2½ x 22in
(6.5 x 56cm), from one fabric or
four, one for each side of the quilt

QUILTING THREAD
Cotton perlé no.12, variegated

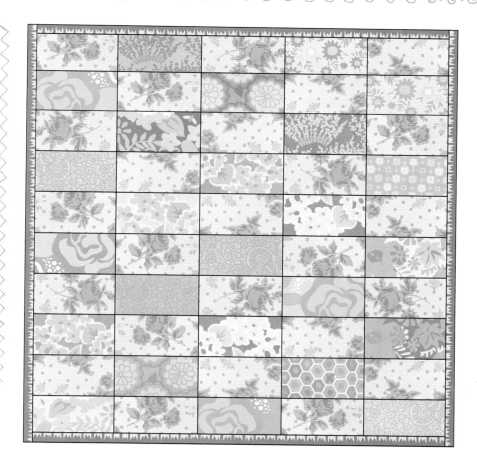

METHOD

1   Lay out the rectangles in ten rows of five, with the short sides of each rectangle touching. Alternate the two types of rectangle fabric, as shown in the patchwork pattern above.

2   Machine stitch the rectangles together row by row, pressing the seams in alternating directions as you go.

3   Stitch the long rows together, long side to long side, to form a square. You should not need to pin as the seams will lock together to form a neat join. Press the seams open.

4   Layer the patchwork with backing and wadding (batting), and use your favourite method to baste.

5   I used big-stitch quilting, working in straight lines ¼in (5mm) in from each seam.

6   When the top is quilted, trim the surplus backing and wadding (batting) and bind using the method given on pages 24–25.

NINE-PATCH QUILT

18½ x 26½in (47 x 67cm)

There are endless ways to use the simple nine-patch block in quilt-making, and creating little quilts makes seeing the results a quick and easy process. Perhaps you will be inspired to start working on a series of these to hang on your wall. In this quilt I wanted to introduce a larger scale print, and the big squares were the ideal place to do it.

YOU WILL NEED

NINE-PATCH BLOCKS
Dark fabric: 50 x 2½in (127 x 6.5cm), cut into
 twenty 2½in (6.5cm) squares
Light fabric: 62½ x 2½in (159 x 6.5cm), cut into
 twenty-five 2½in (6.5cm) squares

LARGE PATCHES
Four squares, 6½ x 6½in (16.5 x 16.5cm)

BORDERS
Fabric A: cut two strips, 18½ x 2½in (47 x 6.5cm)
Fabric B: cut two strips, 18½ x 2½in (47 x 6.5cm)

BACKING
28 x 20in (71 x 51cm)

WADDING (BATTING)
28 x 20in (71 x 51cm)

BINDING
Two strips, 2½ x 28in (6.5 x 71cm)
Two strips, 2½ x 20in (6.5 x 51cm)

QUILTING THREAD
Cotton perlé no.12, variegated

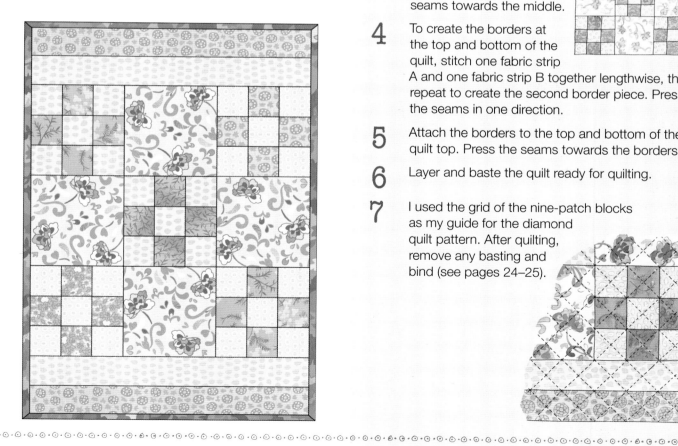

METHOD

1 Alternate dark and light fabric squares and stitch them together in blocks of nine: create three rows of three alternating squares for each block, pressing the seams towards the darkest fabric each time you sew. Stitch the three alternating rows together to create your nine-patch square. Press the seams towards the centre of the block. Repeat four more times to create five nine-patch blocks.

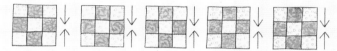

2 Lay out the nine-patch blocks and the large squares, alternating them to create a three-by-three square. Stitch the nine-patch squares and the large squares together in rows of three, pressing the seams towards the large squares.

3 Sew the three rows together, and press the seams towards the middle.

4 To create the borders at the top and bottom of the quilt, stitch one fabric strip A and one fabric strip B together lengthwise, then repeat to create the second border piece. Press the seams in one direction.

5 Attach the borders to the top and bottom of the quilt top. Press the seams towards the borders.

6 Layer and baste the quilt ready for quilting.

7 I used the grid of the nine-patch blocks as my guide for the diamond quilt pattern. After quilting, remove any basting and bind (see pages 24–25).

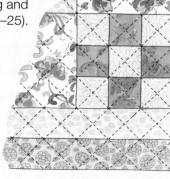

HIDDEN CROSSES QUILT

18 x 22in (46 x 56cm)

I was enchanted by a small quilt from the collection of Mary Ghormley. It was made around 1910 from simply pieced nine-patch blocks, but the addition of the centre square in the sashing creates a secondary pattern. This quilt lends itself to the use of scraps. Save enough pieces close in colour and pattern to keep the optical effect.

YOU WILL NEED

RED FABRIC
Nine-patch squares:
40 x 2½in (102 x 6.5cm),
cut into sixteen 2½in
(6.5cm) squares
Sashing: 26 x 2½in
(66 x 6.5cm), cut into
four 2½ x 6½in
(6.5 x 16.5cm) rectangles
Single border: cut two strips,
2½ x 14½in (6.5 x 37cm)
Double border:
Fabric A: cut two strips,
18½ x 2½in
(47 x 6.5cm)
Fabric B: cut two strips,
18½ x 2½in
(47 x 6.5cm)

WHITE FABRIC
Nine-patch squares:
52½ x 2½in
(133.5 x 6.5cm), cut into
twenty-one 2½in (6.5cm)
squares

BACKING
20 x 24in (51 x 61cm)

WADDING (BATTING)
20 x 24in (51 x 61cm)

BINDING (OPTIONAL)
Four strips, 24 x 2½in
(61 x 6.5cm)

QUILTING THREAD
Cotton quilting thread no.40

METHOD

1 Alternate red and white fabric squares and stitch them together in blocks of nine: create three rows of three alternating squares for each block, pressing the seams towards the red fabric each time you sew. Stitch the three alternating rows together to create your nine-patch square. Press the seams towards the centre of the block. Repeat three more times to create four nine-patch blocks.

2 Stitch a nine-patch block to each long side of a sashing strip. Press towards the sashing strip. Make two.

3 Stitch the remaining white square between the two ends of the two remaining sashing strips. Press towards the sashing strip.

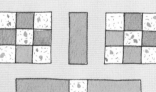

4 Assemble, pressing the seams towards the sashing strips each time.

5 On two opposite sides of the square, attach the lengths of single border fabric. Press the seams towards the border.

6 Stitch one A and one B strip together along their long sides and press in one direction. Repeat to create a second pair. Attach these double borders to the remaining two sides of the square and press outwards towards the border.

7 For a turn-through finish, see pages 26–27. If you want to bind your quilt, layer and baste the backing and wadding (batting) together.

8 Mark the quilting. I quilted ¼in (5mm) from the finished edge of the quilt first. I used the grid of the nine patch blocks as my guide to mark the diagonals, and stopped where the blocks stopped. This makes a diamond grid in the centre of the quilt. If binding see pages 24–25.

DIVIDED NINE-PATCH QUILT

17½ x 17½in (44.5 x 44.5cm)

Stitching nine-patch blocks is fun and easy,
but cutting them up and rearranging them
makes for even more great ideas.

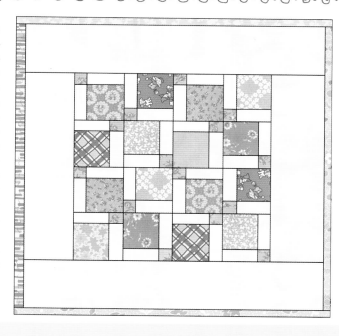

YOU WILL NEED

FOR FOUR NINE-PATCH BLOCKS
Four yellow squares, 2½ x 2½in (6.5 x 6.5cm)
Sixteen white squares, 2½ x 2½in (6.5 x 6.5cm)
Sixteen scrap squares, 2½ x 2½in (6.5 x 6.5cm)

BORDER
Two strips, 3½ x 11½in (9 x 29.5cm)
Two strips, 3½ x 17½in (9 x 44.5cm)

BACKING
20 x 20in (51 x 51cm)

WADDING (BATTING)
20 x 20in (51 x 51cm)

BINDING
Four strips, 2½ x 20in (6.5 x 51cm)

QUILTING THREAD
Cotton quilting thread no.40

METHOD

1 Lay out four nine-patch blocks with a yellow square in the centre and different scraps in each corner. Stitch together and press towards the print fabric; press the long seams open. Make four.

2 The block should measure 6½in (16.5cm) now, including the seam allowance. You need to cut the block into quarters. Either measure 3¼in (8.25cm) from the raw edges to cut or 1in (2.5cm) from the internal seams in both directions. Cut all of the blocks into four.

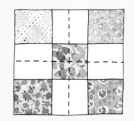

3 Rearrange the cut pieces to create the new design.

4 Stitch the design together, pressing the seams open as you go; sew the squares together in pairs, then sew the pairs to make a larger square. Make four of these blocks.

5 Lay the blocks out in two rows of two, and stitch together to create the centrepiece of the design. Press the seams open.

6 Now add the borders. Stitch the shortest two on opposite sides of the quilt. Press the seams towards the borders. Then add the remaining two borders to the top and bottom of the quilt. Press towards the borders.

7 Layer and baste together with the backing and the wadding (batting).

8 Mark the quilting design. I used the grid of the patchwork to gauge the design. Note that not all of the diagonal lines extend into the border.

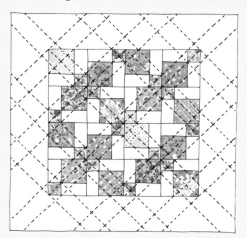

9 When quilted, remove any remaining basting and bind the quilt. See pages 24–25.

SCRAP PRESERVER QUILT

16½ x 14½in (42 x 37cm)

Just when you think every last piece of your favourite
fabric is gone for good, there will always be a piece you
can put in a quilt like this. I sometimes make these to
remember a special full-sized bed quilt, just to recall the
palette that I loved working with.

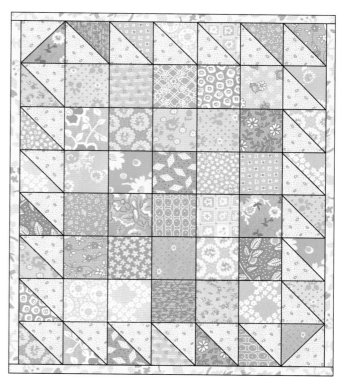

YOU WILL NEED

METHOD

1 Lay out your squares in six rows of five squares.
To check to see how well they blend together
try either of these easy design tips. Look at the
layout through the viewfinder on your camera.
This often shows up things that you don't notice
when looking directly at the fabrics. The other
thing to try is looking at your layout through a
sheet of clear red plastic. You can often buy this
in stationery shops as an A4 sheet or a file insert.
Looking through this only lets you see the value,
not the colours. If any squares stand out they
might need replacing.

2 To make the border pieces, place a light and
medium fabric triangle right sides together and
stitch along the bias side. You can chain piece
for speed (see page 18). Make twenty-six pairs,
pressing the seams open.

3 Position these two-tone squares around the
edges, and check again for blending.

4 Stitch the squares in each row together.
The first and last row will be all triangle units,
the rest will just have a triangle unit at each end.
Sew eight rows. Press the seams in alternating
directions across each row.

5 Stitch the rows
together and press
the seams open.

6 Layer and baste with
wadding (batting) and
backing fabric. This
quilt also looks good
if you use the turn-through method
of finishing (see pages 26–27).

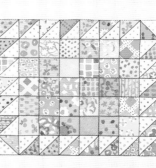

7 Mark the quilting grid. Note that the cross hatching
appears in the central squares but at the triangle
border the quilting runs in the ditch of the triangles
only. After quilting, remove any basting and bind
the quilt. See pages 24–25.

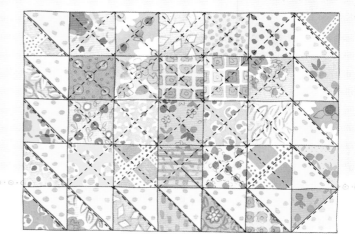

SOFT AND FADED VINTAGE QUILT

23 x 23in (58.5 x 58.5cm)

Old quilts are often my inspiration, as I will translate them into new colourways. This one appealed because of its softly faded appearance. Not all fabrics will fade at the same rate and this often leads to one or two standing out a little more. Play with this idea in the nine-patch blocks to create some different looks.

Fading fabrics

If the fabrics you want to use are not faded enough, try using the back of them instead as this often tones down the design, depending on the printing process. Or, you could use a bleach bath to soften the colours. Always work in a well-ventilated space using gloves and protective clothing. I use one bucket of cold water with a cup of bleach in it and another bucket of cold water with a cup of vinegar (or use a commercial dye-stop product of your choice). Transfer the fabrics between the two buckets until you have the desired result, then rinse thoroughly and wash in the washing machine with your usual detergent.

YOU WILL NEED

FOUR NINE-PATCH BLOCKS
Twenty 2½in (6.5cm) squares
Thirty-two 2½ x 3in (6.5 x 7.5cm) strips, cut into half square triangles using a specialist half square triangle cutting ruler or the template on page 124

BORDER
Two strips, 4½ x 15½in (11.5 x 39.5cm)
Two strips, 4½ x 23½in (11.5 x 60cm)

SASHING
Two strips, 3½ x 6½in (9 x 16.5cm)
One strip, 3½ x 15½in (9 x 39.5cm)

BACKING
25 x 25in (63.5 x 63.5cm)

WADDING (BATTING)
25 x 25in (63.5 x 63.5cm)

BINDING
Four strips, 25 x 2½in (63.5 x 6.5cm)

QUILTING THREAD
Cotton quilting thread no.40

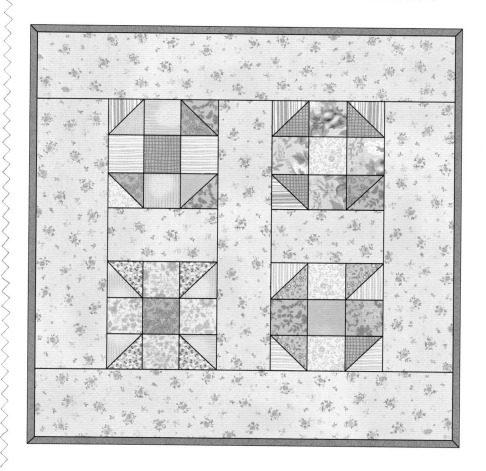

METHOD

1   Lay out the four patchwork blocks, as shown right.

2   Make the half square triangle patches first. Stitch the triangles together right sides facing and press the seams open.

3   Stitch together your nine-patch blocks. Sew together the top and bottom rows of each block first, pressing the seams inwards towards the central square. Sew the middle row last, pressing the seams outwards from the central square. Stitch together the three rows of each nine-patch block, pressing the seams down from the top and up from the bottom, towards the middle row.

4   Sew a short sashing strip between pairs of blocks and press towards the sashing. Then sew the long sashing strip between the two rows and press towards the sashing.

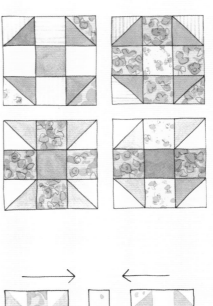

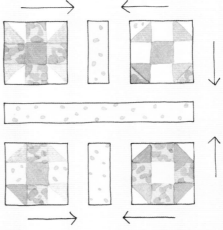

5   Add the short borders first to opposite sides and press out towards the borders. Then, stitch the longer borders on to the top and bottom of the design, pressing out towards the borders.

6   Layer and baste the quilt with backing fabric and wadding (batting).

7   Mark the quilting by starting in the corner of the quilt and marking in 1in (2.5cm) increments. The lines cross over in the main part of the quilt, but not on the borders.

8   Remove the tacking and prepare the quilt for binding. See pages 24–25.

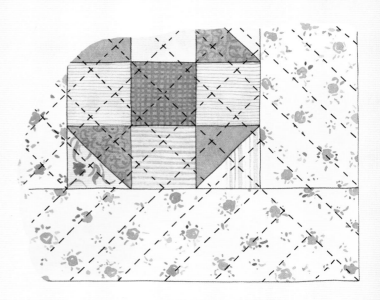

NINE-PATCH SAMPLER QUILT

26½ x 34½in (67 x 88cm)

Sometimes there are just too many fun blocks and combinations of fabrics to try out, and there is no time to make a quilt from each one. So a sampler quilt is the perfect solution. Each block can be showcased and yet works together to make a coherent quilt.

YOU WILL NEED

NINE-PATCH BLOCKS

Block 1:
Light: five 2½in (6.5cm) squares
Medium: four 2½in (6.5cm) squares

Block 2:
Light: four 2½in (6.5cm) squares, four
strips 2½ x 3in (6.5 x 7.5cm) for the
half square triangles
Medium: four strips 2½ x 3in (6.5 x
7.5cm) for the half square triangles,
one 2½in (6.5cm) square

Block 3:
Light: two 2½in (6.5cm) squares, six
strips 2½ x 3in (6.5 x 7.5cm) for the
half square triangles
Medium: one 2½in (6.5cm) square,
six strips 2½ x 3in (6.5 x 7.5cm) for
the half square triangles

Block 4:
Light: two 2½in (6.5cm) squares, four
strips 2½ x 3in (6.5 x 7.5cm) for the
half square triangles
Medium: one 2½in (6.5cm) square, four
strips 2½ x 3in (6.5 x 7.5cm) for the
half square triangles

Block 5:
Light: three 2½in (6.5cm) squares
Medium: three rectangles 2½ x 4½in
(6.5 x 11.5cm)

Block 6:
Light: four 2½in (6.5cm) squares, four
strips 2½ x 3in (6.5 x 7.5cm) for the
half square triangles
Medium: one 2½in (6.5cm) square, four
strips 2½ x 3in (6.5 x 7.5cm) for the
half square triangles

Block 7:
Light: four 2½in (6.5cm) squares, four
strips 2½ x 3in (6.5 x 7.5cm) for the
half square triangles
Medium: four strips 2½ x 3in (6.5 x
7.5cm) for the half square triangles,
one 2½in (6.5cm) square

Block 8:
Light: three 2½in (6.5cm) squares, four
strips 2½ x 3in (6.5 x 7.5cm) for the
half square triangles
Medium: two 2½in (6.5cm) squares,
four strips 2½ x 3in (6.5 x 7.5cm) for
the half square triangles

Block 9:
Light: six strips 2½ x 3in (6.5 x 7.5cm)
for the half square triangles
Medium: one strip 2½ x 6½in (6.5 x
16.5cm), six strips 2½ x 3in (6.5 x
7.5cm) for the half square triangles

Block 10:
Light: four 2½in (6.5cm) squares
Medium: two 2½in (6.5cm) squares, one
strip 2½ x 6½in (6.5 x 16.5cm)

Block 11:
Light: four 2½in (6.5cm) squares
Medium: five 2½in (6.5cm) squares

Block 12:
Light: six 2½in (6.5cm) squares, two
strips 2½ x 3in (6.5 x 7.5cm) for the
half square triangles
Medium: one 2½in (6.5cm) square, two
strips 2½ x 3in (6.5 x 7.5cm) for the
half square triangles

Cut half square triangles with a specialist
ruler or use the template on page 124

SASHING
13in (33cm) length of full-width fabric:
cut thirty-one rectangles, 2½ x 6½in
(6.5 x 16.5cm)

POSTS
5in (13cm) length of full-width fabric:
cut twenty 2½in (6.5cm) squares

BACKING
30 x 40in (76 x 102cm)

WADDING (BATTING)
30 x 40in (76 x 102cm)

BINDING
Two strips, 2½ x 40in (6.5 x 102cm)
Two strips, 2½ x 30in (6.5 x 76cm)

QUILTING THREAD
Cotton quilting thread, weight 35

Blocks 1–3, left to right

Blocks 4–6, left to right

Blocks 7–9, left to right

Blocks 10–12, left to right

METHOD

1   When stitching each of the nine-patch blocks together, start by sewing the half square triangles first. Press the seams open.

2   Lay out each nine-patch block as shown below. For each, sew the pieces into three rows. Press the seams in alternating directions. Sew the three rows together and if the seams are bulky, press them open. If not press in one direction.

Blocks 1–6, left to right

Blocks 7–12, left to right

3   Lay out the sashing pieces and posts. Stitch together and press towards the sashing, as shown. Make five rows.

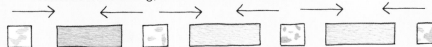

4   Lay out the blocks using the patchwork pattern for guidance and place the sashing pieces in between. Sew the rows together pressing towards the sashing. Make four rows.

5   Arrange the complete quilt alternating sashing rows with block rows and sew together. Press towards the sashing.

6   Layer the quilt top with wadding (batting) and backing fabric and baste together.

7   For this quilt I have used what is known as 'outline quilting'. I quilted ¼in (5mm) in from the seams around all of the medium fabrics. I then quilted ¼in (5mm) in from the seams of the sashing and posts, but in continuous lines.

8   When quilted, remove any remaining basting and bind the quilt as on pages 24–25. When the quilt is bound, complete the quilting by stitching a line ¼in (5mm) in from the binding.

Outline quilting

This type of quilting goes around each shape that you choose. Here I have quilted around all of the medium fabrics in the blocks. You can mark this line with tape or chalk and a ¼in (5mm) ruler, but, as you quilt you will quickly realise that you can quilt this with no marking! You are quilting along the edge of the bulk of the seam allowance, and can feel that with your fingers. Let that guide you and you will save time marking the design.

HOURGLASS QUILT

17½ x 23in (44.5 x 58.5cm)

These square blocks sewn from small triangles have always been a favourite of mine. Stitching them into these little quilts is a great way to experiment. I used one print with quite a large repeat. I love that by cutting it into small pieces you see different things in each block.

YOU WILL NEED

HOURGLASS BLOCKS
Light fabrics, forty-eight strips, 2½ x 3in (6.5 x 7.5cm): cut forty-eight half square triangles using the template on page 124 or a specialist cutting ruler
Medium fabrics: forty-eight strips, 2½ x 3in (6.5 x 7.5cm): cut forty-eight half square triangles using the template on page 124 or a specialist ruler

BACKGROUND
From a 16in (41cm) length of full-width fabric, cut the following:
Six 4½in (11.5cm) squares (A)
Three 7¾in (20cm) squares. Sub-cut these into quarter square triangles – you will need ten of these (B)
Two 3¾in (9.5cm) squares. Sub-cut into four half square triangles (C)

BACKING
19 x 25in (48.5 x 63.5cm)

WADDING (BATTING)
19 x 25in (48.5 x 63.5cm)

BINDING
Two strips, 20 x 2½in (51 x 6.5cm)
Two strips, 25 x 2½in (63.5 x 6.5cm)

QUILTING THREAD
Quilting cotton, 40/3

Setting on point

Instead of lining up horizontal rows of blocks to stitch together, for this quilt the blocks sit on their points. This means that we can still stitch the quilt together in rows, but they are all diagonal, and different lengths (see the diagram on page 50). Setting blocks on point is a great way to make them go further as they make a larger quilt than if you set them in straight rows.

METHOD

1 Start by sewing the half square triangles together in pairs – one light and one medium – to form squares. Press the seams towards the medium fabric.

2 Each block needs four units. Stitch the units together in pairs, pressing the seams in opposite directions.

3 Now sew the pairs together and press the seams in one direction. Make twelve in total.

4 Lay out the blocks with the setting squares (A) and the side triangles (B). The corner triangles (C) can go on last.

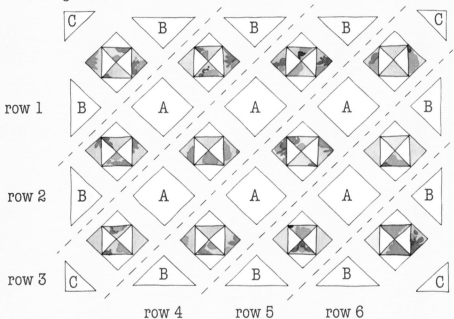

row 1

row 2

row 3

row 4   row 5   row 6

5 Stitch the blocks together to create each row, pressing the seams towards the lighter fabric.

6 Stitch the rows together and press towards the row with the most light squares. Now stitch the corner triangles. To centre them, fold in half along the bias edge and finger press a crease. Line this up with the centre seam on the pieced block. Press towards the corner.

7 Trim off any excess to square up the quilt.

8 Layer and baste ready to quilt. Machine quilt using a pre-programmed wavy stitch. When quilted, remove any basting and bind. See pages 24–25.

FRAMED FOUR-PATCH MEDALLION QUILT

10½ x 10½ in (27 x 27cm)

Lots of quilts rely on a repeat block arrangement, but this little medallion quilt starts with one block in the centre and then builds up with borders or frames. This design reminds me of English stained-glass windows, with its central feature and the circular ripple of quilting.

YOU WILL NEED

FOUR PATCH
Two 2½in (6.5cm) squares in two different fabrics

BORDER TRIANGLES
Colour A: two squares, 3¼in (8.5cm), cut into eight
  quarter square triangles
Colour B: one square 3¼in (8.5cm), cut into four
  quarter square triangles

CORNER TRIANGLES
Four 2½ x 3in (6.5 x 7.5cm) strips: cut four half
  square triangles, using the template on page 124
  or a specialist half square triangle cutting ruler

BORDER
Two 2½ x 6½in (6.5 x 16.5cm) strips
Two 2½ x 10½in (6.5 x 27cm) strips

BACKING
12 x 12in (30.5 x 30.5cm)

WADDING (BATTING)
12 x 12in (30.5 x 30.5cm)

BINDING
Four 2½ x 12in (6.5 x 30.5cm) strips

QUILTING THREAD
Cotton quilting thread no.40

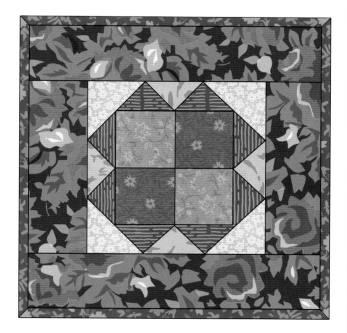

METHOD

1 Stitch the four squares for the centre block, pressing all of the seams open. Sew two together at a time, then sew the two blocks together to create a square.

2 Stitch the border triangles together as shown for the four borders. Press the seams open.

3 Stitch a triangle border to opposite sides of the four-patch, making sure the centre seams match with the centre of the triangle. Press the seams open. Repeat on the other two sides.

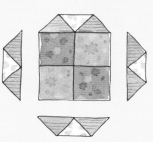

4 Now stitch on each of the four corner triangles. Fold each triangle in half along the bias edge and carefully finger press a crease. Match this up with the intersecting seams on each corner. Press the seams towards the triangles.

5 Stitch the short borders to opposite sides of the patchwork; press the seams towards the border. Now add the remaining long borders to the other two sides and press away from the centre.

6 Layer and baste the patchwork with wadding (batting) and backing fabric. I hand quilted this in circles starting in the centre and getting larger as they moved out. Remove any basting and bind the quilt. See pages 24–25.

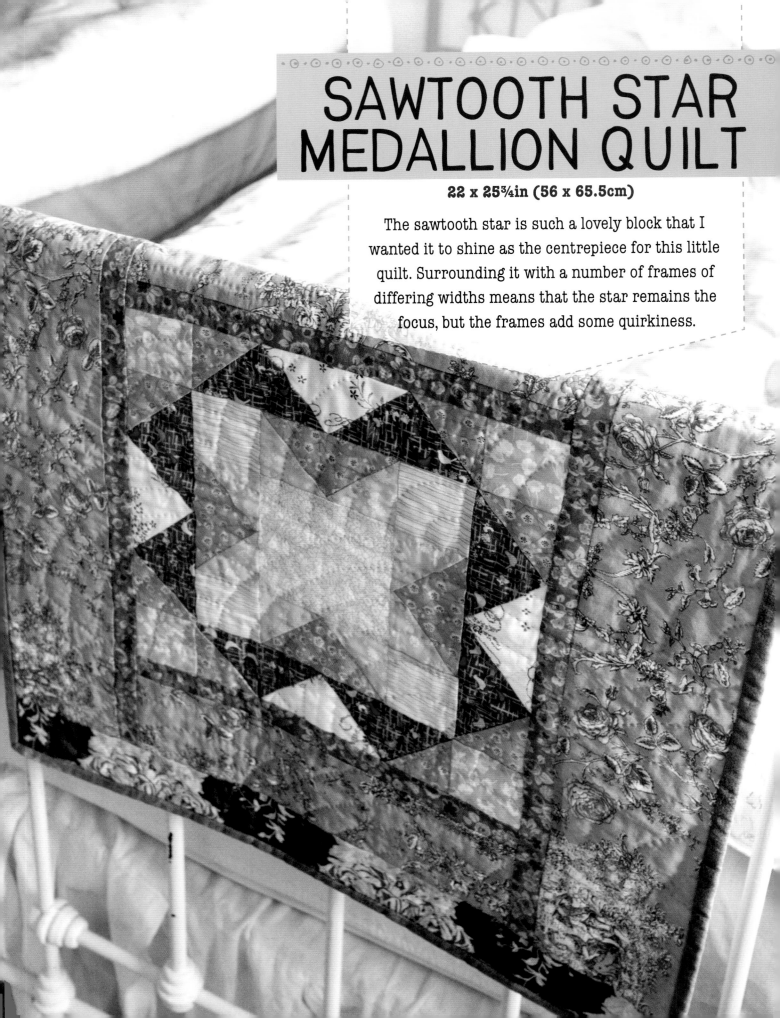

SAWTOOTH STAR MEDALLION QUILT

22 x 25¾in (56 x 65.5cm)

The sawtooth star is such a lovely block that I wanted it to shine as the centrepiece for this little quilt. Surrounding it with a number of frames of differing widths means that the star remains the focus, but the frames add some quirkiness.

YOU WILL NEED

SAWTOOTH STAR
Centre square: one 4½ x 4½in (11.5 x 11.5cm) square
Star points: eight 2½ x 3in (6.5 x 7.5cm) strips: cut eight half square triangles using the template on page 124 or using a half square triangle specialist cutting ruler
Corner squares: four 2½ x 2½in (6.5 x 6.5cm) squares
Side triangles: four 2½ x 5in (6.5 x 13cm) strips. Cut four quarter square triangles using the template on page 124, or use a specialist quarter square triangle rotary cutting ruler

FIRST BORDER
Dark quarter square triangles: eight 2½ x 5in (6.5 x 13cm) strips: cut eight quarter square triangles using the template on page 124, or use a specialist quarter square triangle rotary cutting ruler

Light quarter square triangles: four 2½ x 5in (6.5 x 13cm) strips: cut four quarter square triangles using the template on page 124, or use a specialist quarter square triangle rotary cutting ruler
Light half square triangles: eight 2½ x 3in (6.5 x 7.5cm) strips. Cut eight half square triangles using the template on page 124, or use a half square triangle specialist cutting ruler
Corner squares: four 2½ x 2½in (6.5 x 6.5cm) squares

SECOND BORDER
Fabric A: two 1¼ x 12½in (3.25 x 32cm) strips and two 1¼ x 19½in (3.25 x 49.5cm) strips

Fabric B: two 3½ x 12½in (9 x 32cm) strips and two 3½ x 19½in (9 x 49.5cm) strips

TOP BORDER
One 2½ x 22in (6.5 x 56cm) strip

BOTTOM BORDER
One 4½ x 17½in (11.5 x 44.5cm) strip
One 4½ x 5½in (11.5 x 14cm) strip

BACKING
24 x 28in (61 x 71cm)

WADDING (BATTING)
24 x 28in (61 x 71cm)

BINDING
Two 2½ x 28in (6.5 x 71cm) strips
Two 2½ x 24in (6.5 x 61cm) strips

QUILTING THREAD
Cotton quilting thread, 35 weight

METHOD

1   Stitch the sawtooth star together by following the diagrams given below and right, following the pressing arrows.

 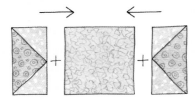 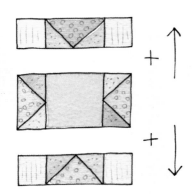

2   Stitch the first border together by making four units as shown below.

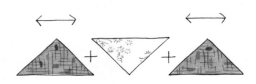 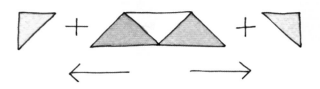

3   Attach the corner squares to two of these border pieces.

4   Sew the shortest two of the four borders onto opposite sides of the star. Press towards the border.

5   Sew the remaining longer borders onto the remaining two sides.

6   Join the second borders together in pairs, fabric A to fabric B. Attach a shorter pair to the top and bottom of the quilt. Press outwards. Stitch the remaining second borders to the remaining opposite sides. Press outwards.

7   Join the bottom border pieces on the short edge. Attach the top and bottom borders to the patchwork. Press away from the centre.

8   Layer and baste the top with backing fabric and wadding (batting).

9   Use the Amish wave template (given on page 22) to hand quilt.

10   When quilted, remove any basting and bind the quilt, see pages 24–25.

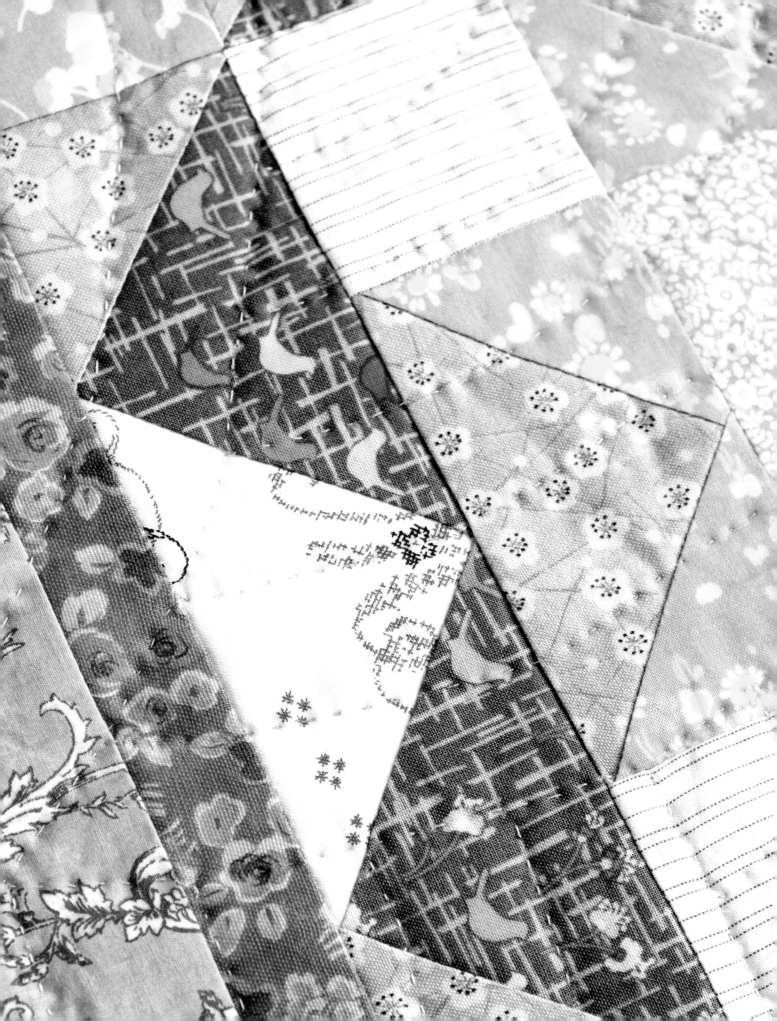

LOG-CABIN QUILT

20 x 20in (51 x 51cm)

Log-cabin blocks are a great way to use up lots of odds
and ends. Using the full strip width of 2½in (6.5cm)
can make the blocks a little bland, but if you cut the strips
in half down the centre, the resulting width gives great
results and allows for more fabrics to be used in each block.

Folklore has it that the centre square represents
the fireplace in the cabin, and the half light/half dark
fabrics, the light and the shadow that the fire casts.
For maximum effect in your quilt, be sure to have a
good contrast between your fabrics.

YOU WILL NEED

CENTRE SQUARE
Four 2½ x 2½in
(6.5 x 6.5cm) squares

LIGHT STRIPS
Minimum of six strips 2½in
(6.5cm) x width of fabric:
each block needs ten logs, so if
you have a lot of scraps, use ten
different fabrics. Cut each fabric
along the length through the
middle, yielding two strips 1¼in
(3.25cm) wide

DARK STRIPS
Minimum of six strips 2½in
(6.5cm) x width of fabric: each
block needs ten logs, so if you
have a lot of scraps, use ten
different fabrics. Cut each fabric
along the length through the
middle, yielding two strips 1¼in
(3.25cm) wide

BACKING FABRIC
22 x 22in (56 x 56cm)

WADDING (BATTING)
22 x 22in (56 x 56cm)

BINDING
Four strips, 22 x 2½in
(56 x 6.5cm)

QUILTING THREAD
Cotton quilting thread no.40

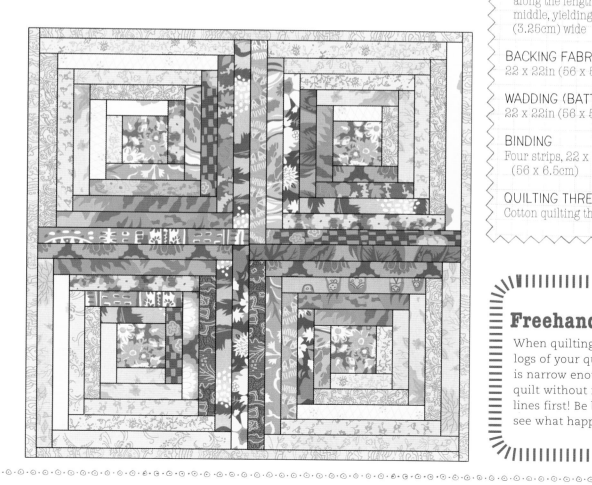

Freehand quilting

When quilting along the
logs of your quilt, the area
is narrow enough for you to
quilt without marking the
lines first! Be brave, and
see what happens.

METHOD

1   You will be working in rounds, stitching strips around the central square. You can measure each log and cut it to length then stitch, but I must admit that for this I simply sew the logs in place and trim them just before I finish stitching. You will be pressing the block after each round, so you will be able to keep them nice and square.

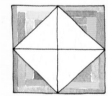

2   Start by stitching a light strip to the centre square. Press all seams for these blocks away from the centre.

3   Continue by adding a second light strip on the next adjacent side of the central square; press.

4   Using a dark strip, sew along the next side; press. On the final side, stitch a dark strip; press – see right.

5   Continue sewing two light strips and two dark strips in rounds until you have completed five circuits, then repeat for the other three central squares.

6   I placed my four blocks with the dark corners touching in the centre of the quilt, see below, far left. Look at the other options and stitch the arrangement you prefer.

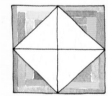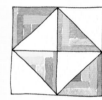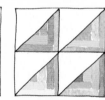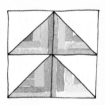

7   Stitch the blocks together in pairs, pressing the seam allowance to one side.

8   Then stitch the two pairs of blocks together, pressing the seam allowance to one side.

9   Layer the patchwork with wadding (batting) and backing fabric and baste together.

10   Quilt down the centre of each log. When complete, remove any basting and bind the quilt, see pages 24–25.

HEXAGON FLOWERS QUILT

15½ x 17¼in (39.5 x 44cm)

If you thought that hexagons sewn over papers were not for you, but still want to stitch a hexagon quilt, you can do that now! This little quilt grows fast with machine piecing. It may even become so addictive that you progress to a full-sized quilt in no time.

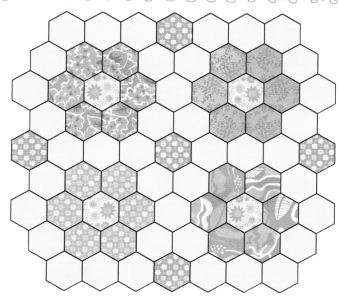

YOU WILL NEED

FOUR FLOWERS
Each flower needs six
2½ x 3in (6.5 x 7.5cm)
pieces for the petals and one
2½ x 3in (6.5 x 7.5cm) piece
for the centre

BACKGROUND
7½ x 40in (19 x 102cm),
cut into 2½ x 3in
(6.5 x 7.5cm) strips, to cut
forty hexagon shapes from
Forty strips, 2½ x 3in
(6.5 x 7.5cm)

GREEN HEXAGONS
5 strips 2½ x 3in
(6.5 x 7.5cm)

BACKING FABRIC
20 x 22in (51 x 56cm)

WADDING (BATTING)
20 x 22in (51 x 56cm)

QUILTING THREAD
Cotton quilting thread
no.40

METHOD

1   Use the template given on page 124 to cut out the hexagons. Use a bradle or something similar to make the small holes at the ¼in (5mm) seam allowance points on the template. Mark the ¼in (5mm) seam allowance points at each corner with a sharp pencil on the wrong side of each hexagon.

2   Now arrange the hexagons in rows, to match the pattern given above.

3   Start stitching the hexagons together right sides facing in rows, from dot to dot. Leave some trailing thread as this will stop the stitches coming undone. You might also want to use a smaller stitch than usual. As you stitch each row, press the seams open.

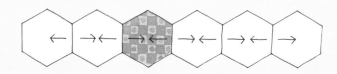

4   When you stitch the rows together you will be setting the hexagons into each other. For this you will need to pivot at the seam points. Take two rows and with the right sides facing, stitch from dot to dot or open seam.

5   When you reach the point to turn, leave the needle in the work and lift the machine presser foot. Keeping the bottom piece flat, turn the top strip to align the raw edges.

6   The needle will act as a pin to keep everything in place. Now lower the foot and continue sewing until you reach the next point or open seam. You will do the same all the way along the seam. Press the seams in alternating directions. As you stitch the rows together the design comes together too.

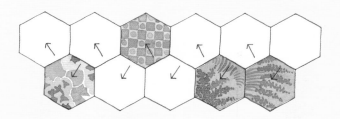

7   When it is complete, layer with backing, wadding (batting) and patchwork as per the turn through method of finishing (see pages 26–27). This works really well for this quilt as there are then no tricky corners to bind.

8   Machine around the edges leaving an opening, trim off the excess backing and wadding (batting) and turn right side out. Remember to snip into the corners before you do so, so that it will turn through neatly.

9   Stitch up the opening and baste around the outside edge. Baste the quilt to keep things in place and then outline quilt around each of the hexagons. Remove the basting when the quilting is finished.

ZIGZAG DIAMONDS QUILT

18 x 19½in (46 x 49.5cm)

This quilt is so much fun, because depending on which way
you hang it you either have zigzags or rows of 3-D cubes.
Make sure you have good definition between the light,
medium and dark fabrics for it to work best.

YOU WILL NEED

DIAMONDS
In light, medium and dark fabrics, cut thirty strips, 2½ x 4½in (6.5 x 11.5cm) – cut thirty diamonds from each of the three colours using the 60-degree diamond template on page 124, or the 60-degree angle line on your cutting ruler, measuring 2½in (6.5cm) between each cut

BACKING
23 x 23in (58.5 x 58.5cm)

WADDING (BATTING)
23 x 23in (58.5 x 58.5cm)

BINDING
Four strips, 2½ x 23in (6.5 x 58.5cm)

QUILTING THREAD
Cotton perlé size 12

METHOD

1 The first thing to do is sew one of each diamond colour together to form a hexagon. Take the medium and dark diamonds and stitch from the raw edge at the narrow point towards the wider angle, stopping at the ¼in (5mm) seam allowance point. Press the seam open. Now place the light diamond ready to set in, starting to sew at the raw edge, with the light diamond on the base of the machine. Sew towards the pressed-open seam and stop when the needle is in the middle. Lift the presser foot, and pivot the top piece around so that the next diamond's raw edges align with the light diamond underneath. Lower the presser foot and continue stitching along the second seam. Press the seam towards the dark and medium fabrics. Make thirty of these.

2 Stitch these hexagons together into six rows of five. Stop and start at the ¼in (5mm) seam allowance points. Press the seams open.

3 Now stitch the rows together as for the hexagon flowers quilt on pages 62–63.

4 Using the diagram below, trim off the excess to square up the quilt. You can, if you want, leave this until you have quilted, before you bind the quilt. Layer and baste the quilt together with the backing and wadding (batting).

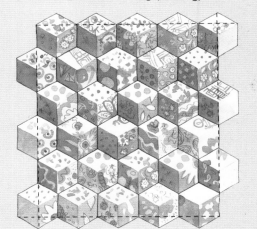

5 I outline quilted the light diamonds and quilted along the zigzags of the blue diamonds with big-stitch quilting and cotton perlé thread.

6 When quilted, remove any basting and bind, see pages 24–25.

WONKY STACKED COINS QUILT

19½ x 27in (49.5 x 69cm)

'Chinese coins' or 'stacked coins' is a great pattern for using up oddments or for trying out new fabric combinations. The lines are usually horizontal, but making it with the tumbler shape creates a lot more movement.

YOU WILL NEED

TUMBLER SHAPES
Sixty pieces, 2½ x 2¾in
(6.5 x 7cm): cut sixty
tumblers from assorted
plain fabrics using the
template on page 124. I
chose a mixture, but you
could grade them from
dark to light in one colour
family, or make a rainbow

BLACK SASHING STRIPS
Three strips, 2½ x 18¾in
(6.5 x 48cm)

BLACK BORDER
Two strips, 3 x 18¾in
(7.5 x 48cm)

Two strips, 5 x 20¼in
(13 x 51.5cm)

BACKING
22 x 29in (56 x 74cm)

WADDING (BATTING)
22 x 29in (56 x 74cm)

BINDING
Two strips, 2½ x 29in
(6.5 x 74cm)
Two strips, 2½ x 22in
(6.5 x 56cm)

QUILTING THREAD
Cotton quilting thread
no.40

METHOD

1   Lay the tumbler shapes out in four rows with
    fifteen shapes in each. Alternate the way the
    shapes lay to form a straight row.

2   Stitch the shapes together, along their long sides;
    this will create straight sides to each row. Press
    the seams open.

3   When the rows are complete, trim off each end
    so that they are straight and each measures the
    same length. Trim the sashing strips and the
    narrow border strips so that they all measure the
    same length, too.

4   Lay out the sashing borders and pieced strips and
    stitch together. If it helps, pin at the start and finish
    as well as the mid-point, to help everything match
    up. Press all the seams towards the black fabric.

5   Now add the top and bottom borders and press
    towards the borders.

6   Layer and baste the quilt with backing and
    wadding (batting) ready to quilt.

7   I quilted in wavy lines, a pre-programmed stitch on
    my sewing machine, using the walking foot as my
    spacing guide – see below for further guidance.
    However, this quilt would also look great quilted in
    the same vertical lines but in cotton perlé and big-
    stitch quilting, spaced ½in (1.5cm) apart.

8   Remove the tacking and bind the quilt, see
    pages 24–25.

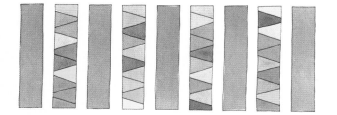

Wavy quilting

Machine quilting in straight lines can sometimes
produce a 'drag' between the rows. To avoid this use
one of the pre-programmed stitches on the sewing
machine. This tends to be more forgiving, and adds
some movement to a quilt design.

BORDERED GARDEN QUILT

16 x 16in (41 x 41cm)

Appliqué is a technique that can help you enhance any patchwork. This simple little quilt takes all of the interest to the borders, and due to the placement of the flowers can hang any way you choose. This works well on a table, too, as the centre is a good size to frame a vase of your favourite blooms.

YOU WILL NEED

CENTRAL SQUARE
12 x 12in (30.5 x 30.5cm)

BORDER STRIPS
Short side A, two strips:
each 2½ x 6½in
(6.5 x 16.5cm)

Short side B, three strips:
2½ x 4in (6.5 x 10cm),
2½ x 5in (6.5 x 13cm),
2½ x 4in (6.5 x 10cm)

Long side A, four strips:
2½ x 2¼in (6.5 x 6cm),
2½ x 5¼in (6.5 x 13.5cm),
2½ x 2½in (6.5 x 6.5cm),
2½ x 7¼in (6.5 x 18.5cm)

Long side B, three strips:
2½ x 8¾in (6.5 x 22.5cm),
2½ x 2½in (6.5 x 6.5cm),
2½ x 5½in (6.5 x 14cm)

NOTE
Although I have given the
sizes of the strips I used,
you can vary this depending
on what fabrics you have
available to you. By changing
the lengths you can use up
all sorts of oddments.

APPLIQUÉ
Leaves, eight 2½ x 3in
(6.5 x 7.5cm)
Flowers, four 2½ x 2½in
(6.5 x 6.5cm)

BACKING
18 x 18in (46 x 46cm)

WADDING (BATTING)
18 x 18in (46 x 46cm)

BINDING
Four 2½ x 18in
(6.5 x 46cm) strips

QUILTING THREAD
Cotton quilting thread,
weight 35

METHOD

1 Stitch the strips together for each of the border edges of the quilt, short side to short side. Press the seams open.

2 Stitch the short borders to opposite sides of the centre square, right sides together. Press the seam towards the centre.

3 Stitch the remaining long borders on and press towards the centre.

4 Make the appliqué shapes: the leaf template can be found on page 124 and instructions on page 19; the flowers should be made as per page 73.

5 Position the appliqué shapes on the centre square. As a guide, the leaves are 1in (2.5cm) up from the border seam and ¾in (2cm) in from the side. Nestle the circle between the leaves. Appliqué down. Once in place, use three strands of embroidery thread to embroider each stem.

6 Layer and baste the quilt top to the backing and wadding (batting).

7 Mark the diagonal quilting lines, starting in each corner, 1in (2.5cm) apart. Note that although the diagonal lines cross over in the centre square to form a grid, they do not in the border. The quilting lines do not cover the appliqué. Instead, before you start quilting the grid, outline quilt approximately ⅛in (3mm) away from the embroidered stem and the leaves and flowers.

8 When the quilting is complete, remove the basting and bind the quilt. See pages 24–25 for guidance on binding.

GIFTS

TECHNIQUES

EMBROIDERY STITCHES

Backstitch

This easy stitch works a stronger outline effect than running stitch. Try to keep the stitches an even length for the best effect. Start at the right-hand end of the line to be covered (left-hand end if you are left-handed). Knot the end of your thread then bring up the needle from the back of the work a stitch length in from the start of the line. Insert the needle in at the end of the line, to the right of your thread, then bring it up a stitch length to the left of your thread. Continue in this way. The stitches on the back will be twice the length of those on the front.

Chain stitch

This stitch can be used effectively as an outline, as it adds more texture than backstitch. Start by knotting your thread and bringing the needle up to the right side of the fabric. Hold the thread in a loop whilst the needle is returned to the point where you started. Then insert the needle up through the fabric, a short distance away but within the loop you just created. Draw the thread up but do not pull tight. Repeat to create a row of chain stitches. On the back you will have an arrow of backstitches.

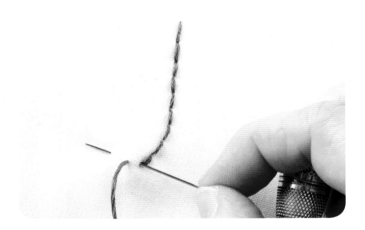

French knots

These little bobbles of thread are great for adding details, such as the dolly's hair on pages 78–81. Knot the end of a piece of thread then bring it up to the right side of the fabric (1). Wrap the thread around the needle twice (2) then insert it back through the hole it came up through (3). Pull it through to create your French knot.

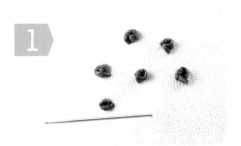

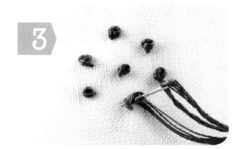

Herringbone stitch

This stitch needs to be worked regularly and closely to cover the raw edges of the fabric you are holding down. One side of the stitch will go through two layers of fabric while the other side will just go through the background fabric. Knot the end of your thread then come up from the back of the work as close to the edge of the appliqué shape as you can. Take the needle down and to the right, then bring it up to the left (1). Overlapping your previous stitch, take the thread over (2) and down through the backing fabric. Bring the needle up to the left (3). Repeat to create a row of overlapping crosses (4). On the back of the work you should end up with two rows of what looks like backstitch.

Work this stitch from left to right if you are right-handed; work right to left if you are left-handed.

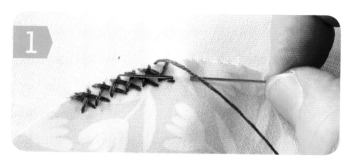

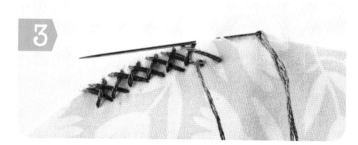

MAKING FABRIC PUFFS

These three-dimensional circles are great for decoration, and are used on the table mat on pages 114–115. Begin by cutting your fabric circles. Knot the end of your thread, then use a running stitch to sew around the edge of each circle (1). When you reach your starting point, pull the thread to draw the circle inwards (2); secure with a few stitches.

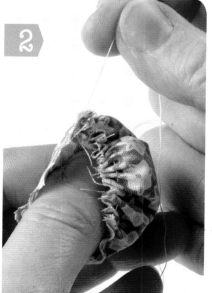

MANX LOG-CABIN MAT

12½ x 12½in (32 x 32cm)

This lovely table mat would be at home in any kitchen or dining room. This method of log-cabin patchwork is historically associated with the Isle of Man. You fold and layer the strips, building up a padded effect but without the use of wadding (batting). As with all log-cabin patchwork, part of the design is created by the contrast between the lighter and darker fabrics used. The design here is built around a centre square, and the strips added on opposite sides. This formation is called 'Courthouse Steps'.

METHOD

1 Place the gridded Vilene onto the linen backing fabric and either tack in place to keep them together or use 505 spray baste.

2 To prepare the strips that will build up around the centre square, fold all the strips in half lengthwise and press, wrong sides together.

3 Take one of the centre square fabrics and place on the gridded Vilene in the centre. It should fit within the gridded lines.

4 Now take the remaining four squares and fold and press each one in half. Place them on top of the flat square, tucking each one under the next so that they all overlap. Pin in place and sew round the outside edge, ¹⁄₈in (0.25cm) away from the raw edge, so that all of them are secured to the Vilene background.

YOU WILL NEED

FABRIC FOR THE CENTRE
Five 2½in (6.5cm) squares

LIGHT FABRICS
172in (437cm) in total from 2½in (6.5cm) strips

(There are twelve rows of strips, so you could use up to twelve different fabrics. Choose fabrics that will blend together and contrast with the dark fabrics. You will cut the strips to length as needed so there is no need to pre-cut them)

DARK FABRICS
189in (480cm) in total from 2½in (6.5cm) strips

(There are twelve rows of strips, so you could use up to twelve different fabrics. Choose fabrics that will blend together and contrast with the light fabrics. You will cut the strips to length as needed so there is no need to pre-cut them)

BACKING
15in (38cm) square of linen and 15in (38cm) square of gridded Vilene (½in/1cm grid)

BINDING
Four strips, 2½ x 14in (6.5 x 35.5cm)

(Choose a darker fabric for the binding. I chose two different types and added them to opposite sides first)

5 Cut two light-coloured folded strips and place on opposite sides of the centre square so that the long folded edge lines up with the second line away from the centre.

6 Stitch these down using a ¼in (5mm) seam allowance measured from the raw edge. You can start and stop with reversing stitches, so as to secure the thread. Trim the ends off on both sides of the work.

7 From the darker fabric cut two folded strips to fit along the remaining opposite sides. Line up with the second line away from the centre square. Machine stitch in place as before.

8 Proceed in this way building up the square design, opposite sides together, until you have twelve rows in place.

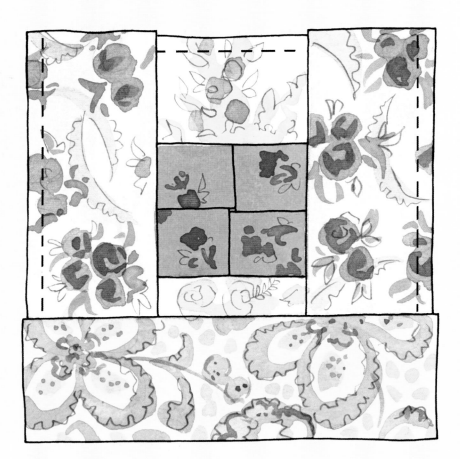

9 Trim the backing fabric to the raw edges and bind the mat using the method on pages 24–25.

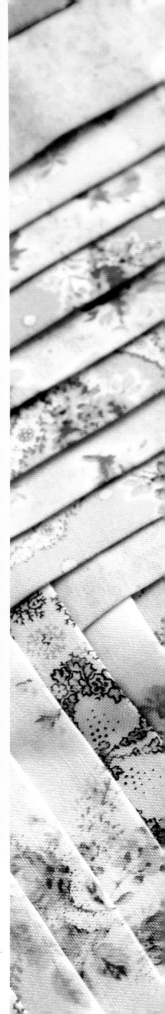

DOLLY

21 x 8in (53.5 x 20.5cm)

Make the dress for dolly from your favourite Jelly Roll™ scraps, transforming them into this cute and cuddly toy. This will be a sure-fire hit with any little person! Why not pair it up with one of the little quilts in the first section to make a truly cosy pair.

YOU WILL NEED

BODY
Calico, 12 x 44in
 (30.5 x 112cm), see
 template on page 125

DRESS
Eight strips, 2½ x 9in
 (6.5 x 23cm)

LEGS
Two strips, 2½ x 10in
 (6.5 x 25.5cm)

ARMS
Two strips, 2½ x 10in
 (6.5 x 25.5cm)

EMBROIDERY THREAD
Stranded cotton
 embroidery floss

ADDITIONAL
Polyester toy stuffing

METHOD

1   You will need to create the template (enlarged to size) given on page 125. Draw around the body template on the front of the calico – create one piece for the front and one piece for the back. Cut out roughly, leaving a margin around the drawn line.

2   Starting at the neckline on the calico front piece, stitch and flip the first strip across the body: position the first strip with the right side facing the head, then sew along the ¼in (5mm) seam allowance attaching the strip to the body. Flip the strip down to cover the top of the body and press.

3   Now attach the next strip. Position it on top of the first strip, right sides facing, and sew through both layers of fabric and the body, about ¼in (5mm) from the bottom edge of both strips. Flip the strip down and press. Continue until all four strips are attached. Replace the template and trim to the exact size of the body. Repeat the process for the back of the body.

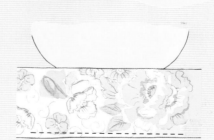

4 Draw facial features onto the front of the face and use a back stitch or chain stitch to make the features using two strands of floss (see page 72).

5 To make the arms and legs, fold the strips lengthwise, right sides together, and sew along the length and across one end. Secure the thread and trim off the excess fabric at the corners. Turn them right side out. For the arms press flat and tie a knot towards the closed end. For the legs, gently stuff with toy stuffing until firm. Leave a ½in (1cm) seam allowance to insert into the body.

6 With the right side of the body facing up, position the arms and legs on top: the raw ends of each should overlap the edge of the doll's body, as shown. Pin or stay stitch them in position, before placing the back piece of the body on top with the right side facing in.

7 Stitch around the edge of the body, leaving a 3in (7.5cm) gap in the middle of one side. Snip the seam allowance at the corners and along the curves. Turn the doll right side out and straighten the limbs. Gently stuff until the body is firm, then slip stitch up the opening.

8 Using six strands of embroidery floss, create French knots along the top of the head's seam line for the hair (see page 72).

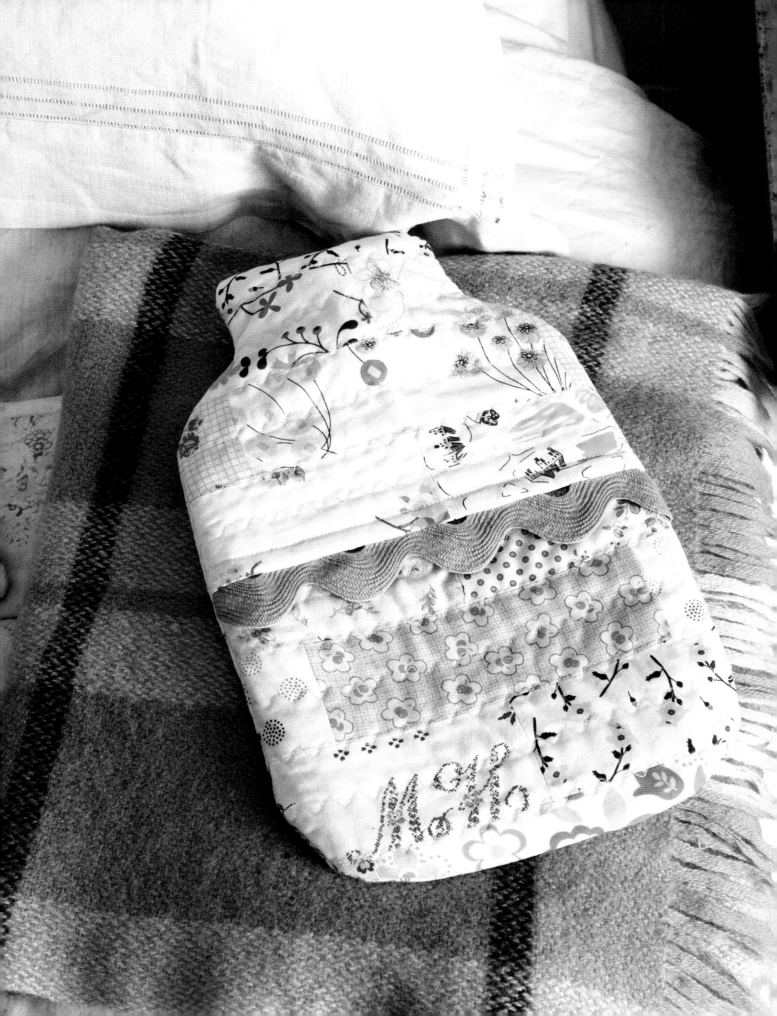

HOT-WATER BOTTLE COVER

14 x 9½in (35.5 x 24cm)

Keep yourself, or a loved one, cosy on those cold winter nights with this easy-to-stitch hot-water bottle cover. Feel very virtuous knowing that you used up your favourite Jelly Roll™ scraps.

YOU WILL NEED

FABRIC
Thirty-two strips, 6½ x 2½in (16.5 x 6.5cm)

LINING
For piece A: 12½ x 14½in (32 x 37cm)
For piece B: 12½ x 10½in (32 x 27cm)
For piece C: 12½ x 8½in (32 x 22cm)

WADDING (BATTING)
For piece A: 12½ x 14½in (32 x 37cm)
For piece B: 12½ x 10½in (32 x 27cm)
For piece C: 12½ x 8½in (32 x 22cm)

QUILTING THREAD
Quilting cotton, 40/3

ADDITIONAL
Ric rac braid, 12in (30.5cm) long, 1½in (4cm) wide

METHOD

1. I used the strips to stitch a quick brick-wall patchwork. The first and all subsequent odd rows consist of stitching two strips together short end to short end. Press the seams open. Make eight of these.

2. To make the even rows, cut a strip in half – you can just fold this and cut with scissors, as it doesn't have to be exact. Stitch each half of this piece to either end of a long strip. Press the seams open and make eight of these.

3. You will use these sixteen rows to create three sections of patchwork. Piece A is made up of seven alternating rows of strips, Piece B has five alternating rows and Piece C has four alternating rows. Don't worry that the rows with a split strip will be slightly shorter, just make sure they balance at either end of the row.

4. Sew the section rows together to create your three different-sized pieces and press the seams open.

5. Layer and baste piece A with wadding (batting) and lining: lay out the lining, face down, place the wadding (batting) on top then the patchwork right side up on top. I quilted along the seams and through the middle of the strips using a wavy pre-programmed machine stitch.

6 For piece C you will need to insert the ric rac edging before quilting. To do this, layer the wadding (batting) and then the lining right side up. Lay the patchwork on top right side down and insert the ric rac along the bottom edge, between the lining and the patchwork. You can line the raw edges up to make this more accurate. Stitch along this edge to hold everything together. Now fold the patchwork over to lay on top of the wadding (batting). Smooth the edge where the ric rac is showing and baste in place ready to quilt. Quilt as for piece A.

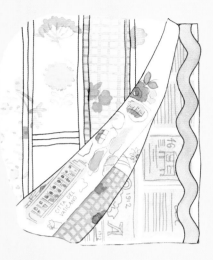

7 To quilt piece B, repeat as for piece C, laying the wadding (batting) down first, the lining next, right side up, then finally the quilt top, right side down. Sew along the top edge to catch the layers together, flip the patchwork over, then quilt.

8 Using the templates (see page 126) cut out the three parts of the cover. For part C and B you will need to position the straight edge next to the already finished edge of the seam.

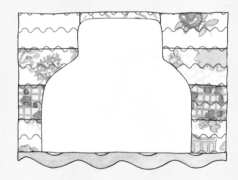
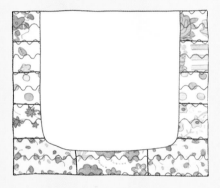

9 Layer your pieces right sides together. Place A down first, right side facing up, then lay C then B on top, right sides facing down. Pin in place around the edge, and sew all of the way around. It may help to use the walking foot on the sewing machine here.

10 Snip at the curves and turn the cover right side out.

COVERED FOLDER

12 x 12in (30.5 x 30.5cm)

A cover like this is a great way to cheer up an old folder, and give it a new lease of life. The sizes given here are for the folder I chose, but it is easy to make the fabric cover any size. Just measure your folder flat and add 1in (2.5cm) to each side to accommodate seams and turnings. Add 6in (15.5cm) at each end for turning and cut a lining the same size as the complete cover.

YOU WILL NEED

TUMBLERS
Each tumbler is cut from strips, 2½ x 2¾in (6.5 x 7cm)

LONG BORDERS
Two strips, 2½ x 23in (6.5 x 58.5cm)

SHORT BORDER FLAPS
Two strips, 13¼ x 5½in (34 x 14cm)

LINING
34 x 13¼in (86.5 x 34cm)

(I used the same cotten-linen blend fabric for the lining, borders and plain tumblers, so in total this is cut from 30in/76cm of fabric)

METHOD

1. Make a template of the tumbler (see page 125) and cut the required number of shapes. You will need to create seventy tumblers in total: twenty-two pairs of tumblers cut from the same patterned fabric, and six tumblers cut from any patterned fabric you like, plus twenty tumblers cut from plain fabric.

2. Lay the tumblers out in ten columns with seven tumblers in each, as per the diagram below – make the first and last row from the tumblers cut from the plain fabric. Pair up the tumblers to make a stretched hexagon design.

3. Stitch the tumblers together in columns, pressing the seams in alternating directions. Sew the columns together, matching up the seams and press these long seams open.

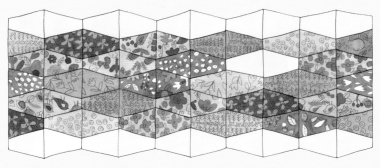

4 Trim off the zigzag edges of the patchwork so that it measures 8½ x 23in (21.5 x 58.5cm).

5 Along the long edges of the patchwork, which will form the top and bottom of the cover, stitch the long plain fabric borders: place the tumbler fabric and the border fabric right sides together, stitch along the edge, taking a ¼in (5mm) seam allowance, then press the seams open.

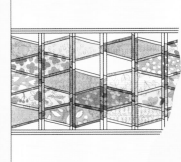

6 In the same way as for step 5, sew the short border flaps to the short ends of the cover. Press the seams towards the plain fabric.

7 Place the patchwork front cover right side facing the right side of the lining and pin all the way round the edge. Start and stop stitching in the middle of a short end, leaving a 2in (5cm) gap in your stitching for turning through. Trim away the excess fabric from the corners. Turn right side out, and slip stitch the opening closed. Press.

8 At each end of the cover, fold the flaps to the front of the cover, turning back 5in (13cm) at each end. (You might need to adjust the size of the turn back depending on the size of your folder. You want the cover to fit snugly).The right sides will be facing. Pin in place and stitch ⅛in (3mm) along the seamed edge, top and bottom. Make sure to secure the stitches.

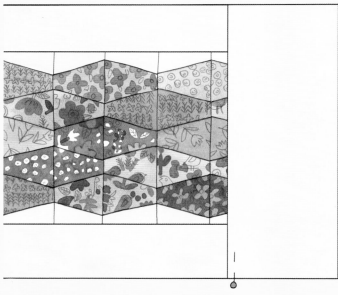

9 Turn right side out and fit over the ends of your folder. It is easiest to do this with the folder open flat.

OLLY THE OCTOPUS

23 x 10in (58.5 x 25.5cm)

Because isn't this what all octopuses are called? Make this for a lucky youngster to spend time with on dry land or even in the bath. Just fill with polyester toy stuffing to make this toy fully washable.

YOU WILL NEED

BODY
Ten strips, 2½ x 10½in (6.5 x 27cm), five for the front and five for the back

WADDING (BATTING)
Two squares, 10½in (27cm)

LINING
Two squares, 10½in (27cm)

EYES
White felt, two pieces, 2½ x 3in (6.5 x 7.5cm)
Black felt, two pieces, 1½ x 1½in (4 x 4cm)

LEGS
Eight strips, 2½ x 16½in (6.5 x 42cm)

QUILTING AND EMBROIDERY THREADS
Machine quilting thread, or cotton perlé if you decide to hand quilt with big-stitch
Black and white cotton embroidery threads for sewing the eyes

ADDITIONAL
Polyester toy stuffing

METHOD

1 Stitch five strips together for both the front and the back of the body. Press the seams open.

2 Layer each with wadding (batting) and lining, with the patchwork on top right side up. Lightly baste together with 505 spray baste or safety pins. Quilt using the seams as your guide with a wavy embroidery stitch selected from the sewing machine. Alternatively, you can quilt by hand using cotton perlé and big-stitch quilting. Quilt the front and the back piece.

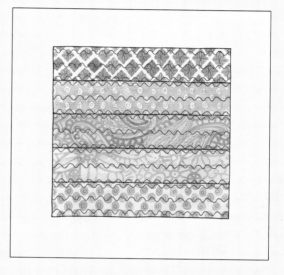

3 Using the template on page 125, cut the white and black pieces of felt for the eyes to shape.

4 Create a circle template with a diameter of 9½in (24cm). On the front piece, draw around the circle template with a Hera marker or use chalk, and use this shape as a guide to place the felt eyes. This will leave a non-permanent mark for your guidance and will not matter if it does not line up perfectly when you stitch the front and back together. Stitch the black felt pupils to the white eyes, then sew onto the body with running stitch.

5 To make the legs, fold each strip right sides together along the length and, starting with securing stitches, sew along one side and across the bottom. Secure to finish and trim away the excess fabric at the corners. Using a chopstick or similar, turn right side out and press flat. Now tie a knot towards the bottom of the leg. Make eight.

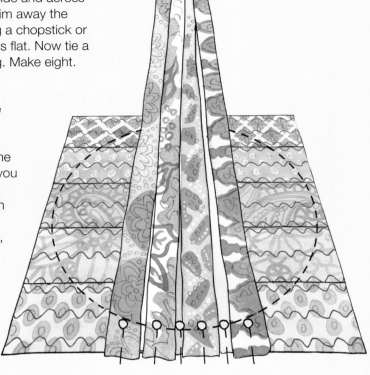

6 Position the legs at the base of the front of the octopus, overlapping them to fit if you do not want them too spread out. Pin them so that the legs will be inside the circle when you stitch the front and back together, leaving about ½in (1cm) for a seam allowance. Stay stitch or tack in place. On the back of the octopus, on the lining, draw around the circle for the body.

7 Place the back of the octopus right sides facing on to the front and pin around the circle. Starting and stopping to one side of the body, sew around the circle, leaving a small gap to turn right side out.

8 Trim the excess fabric away from the circle, leaving a ¼in (5mm) seam allowance. Snip the seam allowance to make the circle smoother when turned through.

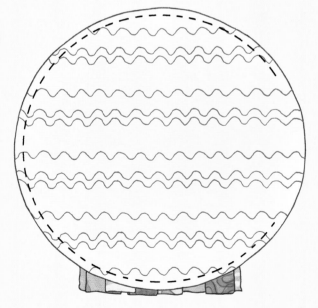

9 Turn right side out and stuff with the polyester stuffing. Slip stitch the opening closed.

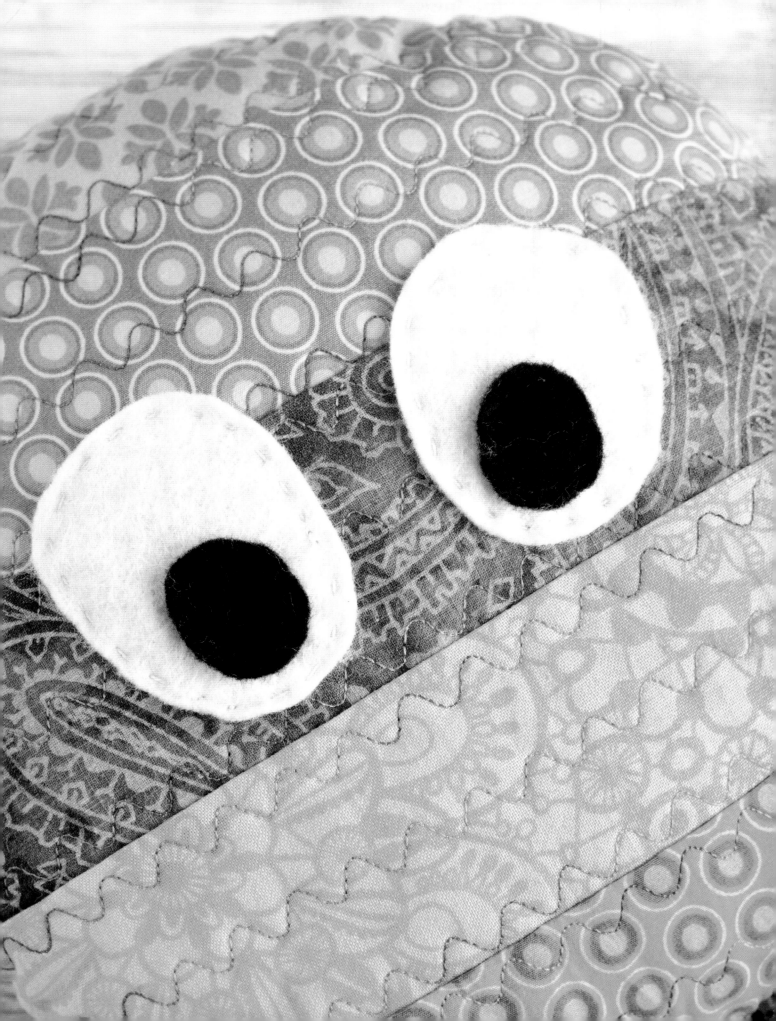

BLUEBIRDS

9 x 6in (23 x 15.5cm)

These chirpy fellows look great hanging in a window, and will brighten up the dullest of grey skies outside. Here I have strung three in a row, but two or four work well too. If you don't want to use wadding (batting) in their wings, coloured felt makes a great alternative.

YOU WILL NEED (PER BIRD)

BODY
Three strips, 2½ x 20in (6.5 x 51cm)

WINGS
Two pieces of wadding (batting) or coloured felt, 2½ x 6in (6.5 x 15.5cm)
Four strips of fabric, 2½ x 6in (6.5 x 15.5cm)
Two buttons, ¾in (2cm) diameter

EYES
Two buttons, ½in (1cm) diameter

ADDITIONAL
Cord for hanging (craft or butchers' cord), 1m (3ft)
Doll needle for threading
Three buttons, ½in (1cm) diameter, to act as optional stoppers
Pinking shears
Cotton quilting thread, no.40

METHOD

1 Stitch the three strips of fabric for the body together along the long sides. Press the seams so that they all lie in the same direction. Fold in half lengthways, right sides together and position the template (see page 127) on top. Pin together to stop the two layers slipping then draw around the template.

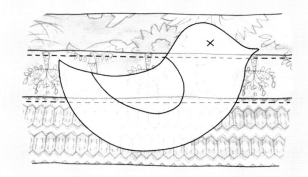

2 Machine along the drawn line, stopping and starting where indicated to leave a turning gap.

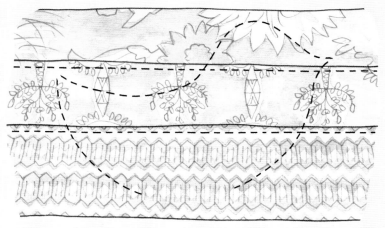

3 Cut out the bird shape leaving a ¼in (5mm) seam allowance, and snip at the curves for smoother turning. Cut away any excess fabric at the beak and tail.

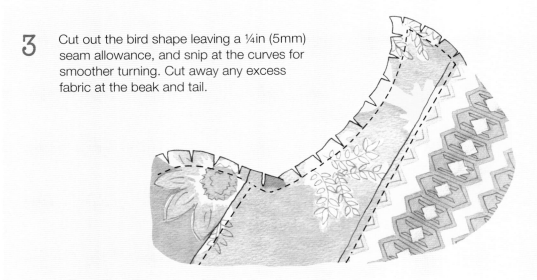

4 Turn right side out and stuff firmly. I use a wooden chopstick to push the stuffing right into the beak and tail. Slipstitch the opening closed.

5 To make the wings, sandwich the wadding (batting) between the two strips of fabric, right sides out. Draw around the wing shape and pin the three layers together. Stitch ¼in (5mm) inside the line. Now cut along the line with pinking shears. Make two.

6 Position the buttons on each wing and sew to either side of the bird's body as indicated. It helps to sew the button onto the wing with a few stitches first so it does not slip when stitching both to the body. Sew one on each side.

7 Position the buttons for the eyes and sew through at the same time, shaping the face slightly as you do so.

8 Make as many birds as you wish. When finished, thread the doll needle with the cord and thread through the body of the bird. If you feel they might slip down, under each bird thread a button through both of the holes to act as a stop, or alternatively tie a small knot. When they are spaced to your liking, tie a loop in the top of the cord for hanging.

ZIPPED POUCH

8 x 6in (20.5 x 15.5cm)

Everyone will be able to find a use for these great pouches. I love using the angled join on the strips as this gives the pouch a bit of a zing! You can position the zip in the middle or a third of the way up, depending on what you think will be most useful.

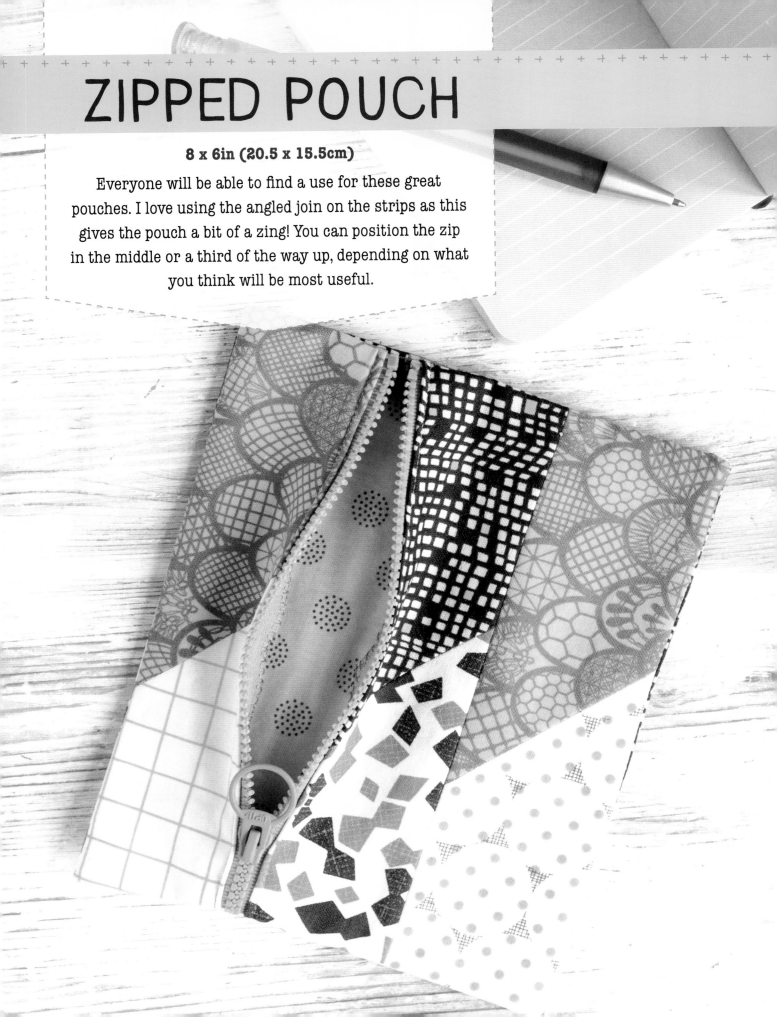

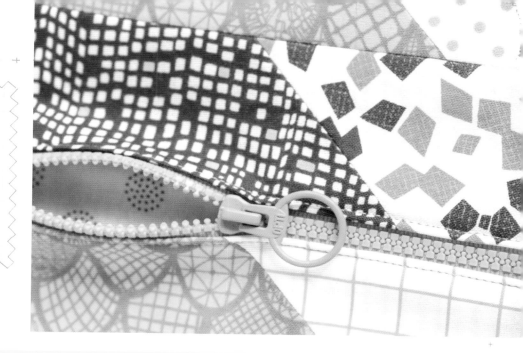

YOU WILL NEED

FABRIC
Six light strips, 2½ x 7in (6.5 x 18cm)
Six dark strips, 2½ x 7in (6.5 x 18cm)

LINING
12½ x 9½in (32 x 24cm)

ADDITIONAL
8in (20.5cm) zip with an open bottom

METHOD

1 Pair up the light and dark strips and overlap them right sides together at right angles, with an extension of about 1/8in (0.25cm). Draw a line with a sharp pencil from indent to indent and stitch along this line.

2 Trim away the excess leaving a ¼in (5mm) seam allowance. Press seam open. Make six.

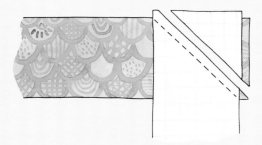

3 Now measure 6in (15.5cm) from the point of the join and trim off the excess. Do this at both ends. The joined strip will now measure 9½in (24cm).

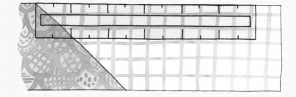

4 Line up the six strips, long edge to long edge, in a pleasing order and stitch together, pressing the seams open.

5 Layer this stitched piece right sides together with the lining fabric. Place one half of the opened zip inside the two pieces, along one short side, with the teeth of the zip inside. The edge of the zip fabric will align with the raw edges of the fabric.

6 Using the zip foot on the sewing machine, stitch along the short edge to secure the zip. Fold the fabric right side out to expose the zip teeth. Smooth this seam and topstitch along the edge.

7 Now close the zip and fold the patchwork and the lining around so that the raw edges line up with the second zip edge. The patchwork will be right sides together with the wrong side of the lining facing you. Pin in place, undo the zip and stitch the zip in as before. Topstitch to finish.

8 Now fasten the zip and turn inside out to sew the side seams of your pouch. At this stage you can decide where you want the zip, either through the middle or a third of the way down.

9 With the zip closed you can now pin and stitch along one end of the pouch. Secure the stitching and then use an overlock stitch or zigzag to neaten. Undo the zip half way and stitch the remaining end of the pouch, secure and neaten in the same way. Turn the pouch right side out and poke out the corners.

LAVENDER RAVIOLI

2½ x 2½in (6.5 x 6.5cm)

These are so much fun to sew and give as gifts. A whole heap can be placed in drawers and in laundry to add that lovely lavender scent. Either cut Jelly Roll™ scraps to size or use the ready-cut mini charms to make them.

YOU WILL NEED

FABRIC
Cut forty-two 2½in (6.5cm) squares

BACKING
Cut forty-two 2½in (6.5cm) squares
  (here I used a strong linen fabric)

THREAD
Bold thread for stitching, such as
  buttonhole twist

ADDITIONAL
Dried lavender, approximately
  2 tsp per ravioli
Jeans sewing needle, for thicker thread
Pinking shears

METHOD

1   Thread up the sewing machine with the bold thread and suitable needle. Adjust the stitch length to something smaller than you usually work with. This is so that when you stitch and then trim, the stitches will not unravel.

2   Sandwich each fabric square with a backing square, wrong sides together, and stitch along one edge. You can chain piece here for speed as the ends do not need finishing off. Snip apart.

3   Repeat until all the squares are sewn together along three of the sides.

4   Use two teaspoons of dried lavender to fill each pocket. Then stitch closed along the fourth side.

5   Finally trim each side with the pinking shears, taking off a fraction so as to neaten but do not trim away too much seam allowance.

HEXAGON PILLOW

19 x 19in (48.5 x 48.5cm)

If you use pairs of half-hexagons, you can create pretty hexagon designs the easy way, working in straight lines on your machine. Use matching pairs of half-hexagons to complete the illusion or select different fabrics to create a wavy pattern.

YOU WILL NEED

FABRIC
To create all sixty half hexagons, you need sixty strips, 2½ x 5½in (6.5 x 14cm)
To make the pattern using twenty-seven whole hexagons, you will need two strips: 2½ x 5½in (6.5 x 14cm) of each colour. Cut twenty-seven pairs from the same fabrics and then six additional single pieces. Alternatively, if you want a scrappier version, use sixty different fabrics

LINING
Calico or muslin, 22 x 22in (56 x 56cm)

WADDING (BATTING)
22 x 22in (55 x 55cm)

BACKING
Two pieces, 22 x 15in (56 x 38cm)

BINDING
Four strips, 2½ x 22in (6.5 x 56cm)

QUILTING THREAD
Cotton thread 40 weight, variegated

ADDITIONAL
Pillow pad, 20 x 20in (51 x 51cm)

METHOD

1   Use the template given on page 125 to cut the half hexagons for the pillow front. Lay out the shapes in ten rows with six half hexagons in each. Pair up the same fabrics to create the complete hexagons, and use the six singles to fill in at the top and bottom row.

2 When you are happy with the layout, start to stitch each row together. Press each row in opposite directions. This way the seams will meet up when the rows are sewn together.

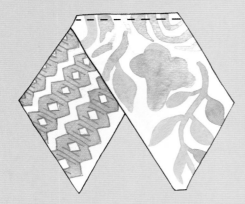

3 Sew the rows together pressing the seams open.

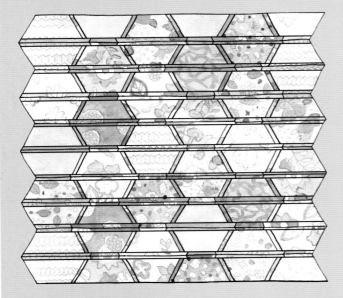

4 Layer the patchwork right side up onto the wadding (batting) and lining fabric. Baste together ready to quilt. I quilted on the machine with a wavy stitch but you can quilt by hand around each hexagon if you wish.

5 When the quilting is complete, remove the basting and trim the patchwork to a 20in (51cm) square.

6 To make the backing pieces, sew a double hem on one of the long 22in (56cm) edges of each of the backing pieces.

7 Lay the pillow patchwork right side facing down on a flat surface. Take the first backing piece and lay it down, right side facing up, with the raw edge aligned with the patchwork's lower raw edge. Take the second backing piece and lay it down so that its long raw edge aligns with the top raw edge of the patchwork. There will be some overlap of the backing pieces. Pin around all the outside edges.

8 Working from the front of the pillow, use the strips to bind the raw edges. See pages 24–25.

9 Stuff with a pillow pad.

FLOWER TABLECLOTH

Size: 40 x 40in (102 x 102cm)

I love linen tablecloths, and this one will brighten up any tea table. Add your favourite tea cups and make a real occasion of it. I used a technique called Broderie Perse to appliqué the leaves here: the shapes, traditionally cut from chintz, are embroidered onto the background using either blanket stitch or herringbone stitch, as I have done here. There are no raw edges to turn under as the stitches cover them in the process. If you are worried about fraying, products are available that can be sprayed on to the fabric edges to strengthen them.

YOU WILL NEED

PETALS
Twenty-eight strips, 2½ x 5½in
(6.5 x 14cm)

TABLECLOTH
42 x 42in (107 x 107cm): use a
hard-wearing cotton-linen blend,
trim the selvedge off and square
up the fabric

ADDITIONAL
Six skeins of black stranded
embroidery floss
Fabric glue basting pen
6in (15.5cm) embroidery hoop

METHOD

1 Using 1in (2.5cm) of fabric, fold a double hem to the wrong side of the tablecloth and tack all the way round. Split a length of the floss into three strands and use this to secure the hem with a running stitch all the way round. Take out the tacking as you go and hide the knots in the hem.

2 Cut your twenty-eight petals out using the template given on page 127.

3 Press the square cloth into quarters on the straight sides and diagonally. These lines will make it easier to place the petals. Place the petals according to the layout shown right, and baste into place with the glue pen.

4 Carefully securing the cloth into the embroidery hoop, use three strands of embroidery thread to work the herringbone stitch around each petal (see page 73), always beginning and ending on a straight side. Work the stitch closely so that it covers the raw edge of the fabric.

5 When all of the petals are in place, follow the manufacturer's instructions to remove the glue. Press the cloth ready for use.

FLOWER-POWER COASTERS

Hexagon: 9 x 7½in (23 x 19cm)
Flower: 11½ x 11½in (29.5 x 29.5cm)

These fun and funky table coasters will brighten up any surface and are large enough for a vase or flowering plant, or for a mug of coffee and accompanying cookie. Make a combination of large and small ones to give as a great set for a new homeowner.

YOU WILL NEED

FABRIC
Hexagon: from one 5in (13cm) square of cotton or linen, cut one hexagon. From six 2½ x 5in (6.5 x 13cm) strips cut six half hexagons
Flower: from one 5in (13cm) square of cotton or linen, cut one hexagon. From twelve 2½ x 5in (6.5 x 13cm) strips cut twelve half hexagons

BACKING
Hexagon: 10in (25.5cm) square
Flower: 13in (33cm) square

WADDING (BATTING)
Hexagon: 10in (25.5cm) square
Flower: 13in (33cm) square
(Use a product such as Insulbright to help make the coasters heat-resistant for use with hot drinks or dishes)

QUILTING THREAD
Cotton perlé no.12 or no.8

METHOD

1   Cut and arrange your fabrics, using the templates on pages 125 and 127. Check that you are happy with the colour scheme.

2   Take one of your half hexagons and with right sides facing, align its top left edge with any of the points on your central hexagon. Stitch from the left hand edge about 1¼in (3.25cm) across its width. Fasten off.

3   Fold the first half hexagon back, but do not press it. Attach the second half hexagon to the next point to the left, and right sides together stitch all the way along the seam. Fold it back.

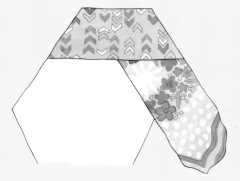

4 Continue around the hexagon, adding the remaining half hexagons, until you are back to the start. Now take the first seam that you only partially stitched, and complete the stitching to the end of the seam. Press the seams away from the central hexagon as you work.

5 If you are making the larger flower, now stitch the petals on. Stitch three on alternating sides of the hexagon, pressing the seams outwards.

6 Then add the last three petals, in the spaces you left at step 5 – start and stop stitching ¼in (5mm) from the raw edge. Press the seams open.

7 To make into coasters, layer with the wadding (batting) and backing fabric: lay a piece of wadding (batting) down first, place the backing on top, right side up, and finally add the patchwork piece, right side down.

8 Stitch all the way around the shape ¼in (5mm) from the edge, leaving a 2in (5cm) space for turning through in the centre of a straight edge. Before turning through, trim the wadding (batting) back to the stitch line and trim the backing to the ¼in (5mm) seam allowance. Trim excess fabric from the corners. For the large flower, snip into the corners.

9 Turn right side out and slip stitch the opening closed. Lightly press if needed.

10 Smooth out the fabric and roll the edges to lie flat. Tack in place around the outside edge. Use the cotton perlé thread to big-stitch quilt the layers together following the outline of the shapes, ¼in (5mm) in from the seams. As you stitch around the outside edge, remove the tacking.

CUT DIAMOND PINCUSHIONS

Small: 5½ x 4½in (14 x 11.5cm)
Large: 8 x 9in (20.5 x 23cm)

Really one can never have too many pincushions, so this little set would make a great gift for the avid stitcher. The dense machine quilting makes them nice and sturdy – it could also be done by hand using big-stitch quilting for a different texture.

YOU WILL NEED

FABRIC
Small: three 2½ x 5in (6.5 x 13cm), light, medium and dark fabrics. Cut one diamond from each

Large: six 2½ x 5in (6.5 x 13cm) strips of light fabric: cut six diamonds
three 2½ x 5in (6.5 x 13cm) strips of medium fabric: cut three diamonds
three 2½ x 5in (6.5 x 13cm) strips of dark fabric: cut three diamonds

LINING
Small: 6 x 6in (15.5 x 15.5cm)
Large: 11 x 11in (28 x 28cm)

WADDING (BATTING)
Small: 6 x 6in (15.5 x 15.5cm)
Large: 11 x 11in (28 x 28cm)

BACKING
Small: 6 x 6in (15.5 x 15.5cm)
Large: 11 x 11in (28 x 28cm)

QUILTING THREAD
Cotton thread, 40 weight

ADDITIONAL
Polyester toy stuffing

METHOD

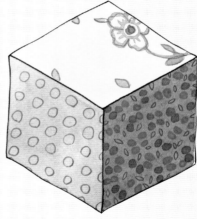

Small pincushion

1   Using the template on page 127, cut your diamond shapes. Following the steps in the Zigzag diamonds quilt on page 65, make one hexagon.

2   Layer the hexagon right side up on top of the wadding (batting) with the lining underneath. Baste together and quilt densely in straight lines ¼in (5mm) apart. Remove basting and trim to the size of hexagon.

3   Place the hexagon right sides together with the backing fabric and machine round the edge, starting and stopping in the middle of a straight side, leaving a small gap.

4   Trim the excess fabric from the corners and turn right side out. Stuff until firm and then slip stitch the opening closed.

Large pincushion

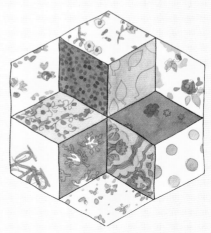

1   Lay out the dark and medium diamonds in a star shape. The star is stitched in two halves. Stitch a medium and dark diamond together. Press the seam open. Now attach the next diamond in the same way. Join the other three diamonds together. Now place the two halves right sides together, pinning in the middle, and stitch across starting and stopping ¼in (5mm) from the edge. Press the seams open.

2   Now taking the light diamonds, set them in around the star as for the small pincushion. You will get a neater finish if you sew alternating diamonds in, press and then fill in the gaps with the last three. Press.

3   Complete the pincushion following steps 2 to 4 for the small pincushion.

BERRIES TABLE MAT

16½ x 27½in (42 x 70cm)

Choose a sunny palette for the barbecue season, oranges and terracotta tones for Halloween and traditional red and green for the Christmas table. The design itself is often seen in antique quilts, and has been given a new lease of life here.

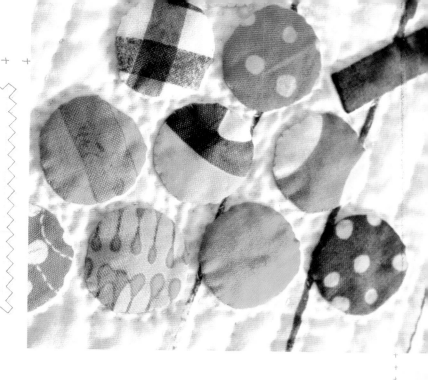

YOU WILL NEED

FABRIC

Berries: forty squares,
2½ x 2½in (6.5 x 6.5cm)

Stalks: two strips, 1 x 8in
(2.5 x 20.5cm)

Background: 16½ x 20in
(42 x 51cm)

Ends: four strips, 2½ x
16½in (6.5 x 42cm)

WADDING (BATTING)
31 x 20in (79 x 51cm)

BACKING
31 x 20in (79 x 51cm)

BINDING
Two different fabrics, one
strip of each, 2½ x 44in
(6.5 x 112cm)

QUILTING THREAD
Cotton quilting thread
no.40, variegated

METHOD

1 From the squares cut out circles for the design: either use the template given on page 125 or just fold the fabric into quarters and trim to a circle. To make the berries, take a length of thread with a knot at the end. Start stitching a small running stitch about ⅛in (3mm) in from the raw edge. Go all the way round, and when you reach the start pull the thread gently to gather up the circle. When pulled up and a circle formed, use a few stitches through the back of the circle to secure the thread. You can now form this into a flat and slightly padded circle. Make forty.

2 Make the stalks by pressing the fabric ¼in (5mm) in on each long side towards the wrong side, so the raw edges meet in the middle. Turn under the ends to neaten.

3 Press the background fabric diagonally into quarters. Use these lines to guide your placement of the overlapping stalks. Pin the stalks in place and appliqué down. Now position the berries. I sometimes position a ruler perpendicular to the end of the stalks to keep the first line of berries straight. Once these are in place build up the rows. Appliqué the berries down.

4 Stitch the end borders together in pairs and press the seam in one direction. Stitch these to each end of the main section of appliqué. Press towards the borders. Layer and baste with the backing and wadding (batting).

5 Quilt around all of the appliqué ¹/₁₆in (1mm) away from the shapes. The background is quilted in straight lines unevenly spaced. Mark these with a chalk wheel or Hera marker, or try quilting them freehand.

6 When complete, bind the edges. See pages 24–25.

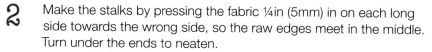

CROCHET HOOK ROLL

18 x 12½in (46 x 32cm)

This cute, colourful crochet roll is perfect for keeping your hooks organised. Choose your own set of colours if you want to personalise it, or consider enlarging the design so that you can store items such as knitting needles or paintbrushes instead.

YOU WILL NEED

INNER LINING
Cotton-linen blend, 18½ x 12½in (47 x 32cm)

OUTER COVER
Cotton-linen blend, 18½ x 12½in (47 x 32cm)
 (I used a plain fabric but you could swap this for a print)

LINING FOR POCKETS
Calico or muslin, 18½ x 6½in (47 x 16.5cm)

POCKETS
Nine strips, 2½ x 6½in (6.5 x 16.5cm)

TIE
One strip, 2½ x 40in (6.5 x 102cm)

EMBROIDERY THREAD
Cotton perlé no.12 for decorative stitching

METHOD

1   To make the pockets, arrange the strips in a line and stitch together, long side to long side. Press the seams open.

2   Place the pocket strip right sides facing onto the pocket lining fabric, and stitch along the top long edge using a straight machine stitch, about ¼in (5mm) from the edge of the fabric. Once secure, flip the pocket fabric over so that the wrong sides are now together, smoothing the seam and aligning the raw edges. Press. Stitch a running stitch ¼in (5mm) from the seamed edge using the cotton perlé.

3   Lay the lining fabric right side up on a flat surface and place the pockets on top, aligning the raw bottom edges. Place the outer fabric on top, right side down, and pin around the top, bottom and right-hand side.

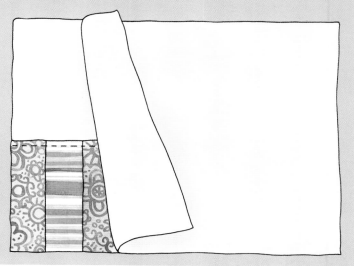

4 To make the tie, fold the strip in half lengthways, wrong sides together, and press. Fold the raw edges in to meet at the fold and press again. Fold in the ends to neaten. Stitch along the folded edge and the ends to secure.

5 Fold the tie in half. To secure it in place you will need to trap the halfway fold under a line of stitching. At the open left-hand side, insert the entire folded tie between your fabric layers, leaving the folded end peeking out between your fabrics, about 4½in (11.5cm) up the left-hand side (see the finished illustration below for guidance). Pin in place and pin the left-hand edge.

6 Stitch around the edges, securing the tie in place as you go, leaving a 2in (5cm) gap in the middle of the top of the rectangle for turning through. Snip the excess fabric away from the corners and turn the whole piece right side out through the gap you left. Slip stitch the gap closed.

7 Press the crochet hook roll. Work out how wide you want your pockets to be and pin them in place accordingly. Using the cotton perlé, stitch along the divisions of the pockets, through all of the layers. Also stitch around the sides and top edge of the lining fabric, ¼in (5mm) from the edge.

8 Slot your crochet hooks into the pockets, turn the flap over at the top and roll the keeper up, lightly securing with the tie.

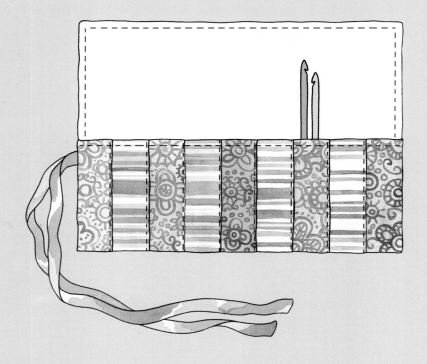

TABLET CASE

Closed: 7¾in x 10½in (20 x 27cm)

Personalise and protect your tablet in style: this lightly quilted pocket will set you apart from the crowd. The measurements given here create a case that will fit a 7¼ x 9½in (18.5 x 24cm) tablet, so you may need to adjust them slightly to fit your chosen model.

YOU WILL NEED

FABRIC
Strips for cover: 116in (295cm) in total: use assorted scraps 2½in (6.5cm) wide and of any length. Stitch them together end to end until you have enough – this is a great way to use up oddments

LINING
11 x 30in (28 x 76cm)

WADDING (BATTING)
11 x 30in (28 x 76cm)

INNER LINING
8½ x 28½in (22 x 72.5cm)

QUILTING THREAD
Cotton quilting thread, no.40

ADDITIONAL
One button, ¾in (2cm) diameter
Narrow elastic, 3in (7.5cm) long: make a loop by knotting the two ends together. Alternatively, use a coloured hair band

METHOD

1   Cut four pieces 20½in (52cm) long, from your long strip of scraps. Stitch together along the long sides. Press seams open.

2   Cut four strips 8½in (21.5cm) long. Sew these together in pairs, long side to long side, pressing the seams open, and then stitch one to each end of the large piece made in step 1. Press the seams open.

3   Layer the lining and wadding (batting), with the patchwork right side up on top, and baste ready to quilt.

4   I quilted in the direction of the strips, along the seams and down the middle using a wavy machine stitch. Trim the wadding (batting) and lining to match the size of the patchwork, and square up if needed.

5 Fold in half widthways, matching the short edge, right sides together; pin and stitch up each long side.

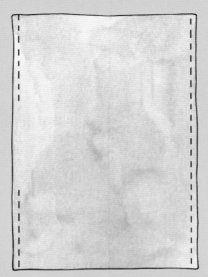

6 To make the lining, fold in half widthways, right sides together. Sew up one side, and on the second side sew to the top, but leave a gap of 2in (5cm) in the middle of the side, for turning through later.

7 Put the lining inside the patchwork, right sides together, matching up the side seams. Pin around the top, and place the elastic in the centre of one side, with the knotted end peeking out, and the loop hidden in between the lining and the patchwork. Pin. Stitch around the top, securing the lining to the patchwork.

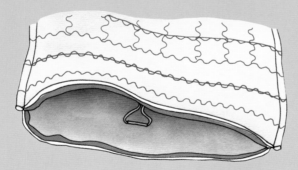

8 Using the gap in the lining, turn through, right sides out. Slip-stitch the opening closed. Push the lining inside the patchwork and pin around the top. Using the same wavy quilting stitch, sew around the top of the case, securing the lining to the patchwork.

9 To position the button, put the tablet inside the case and fold the top over to make a flap. Where the elastic reaches put a pin in to mark. Sew the button in place at the pin mark.

TEMPLATES

The templates shown on pages 124–127 are shown at actual size unless stated otherwise. Simply copy them onto firm card or template plastic and cut neatly around the outline.

TUMBLER FOR
WONKY STACKED
COINS QUILT
pages 66–67

LEAF FOR
BORDERED
GARDEN QUILT
pages 68–69

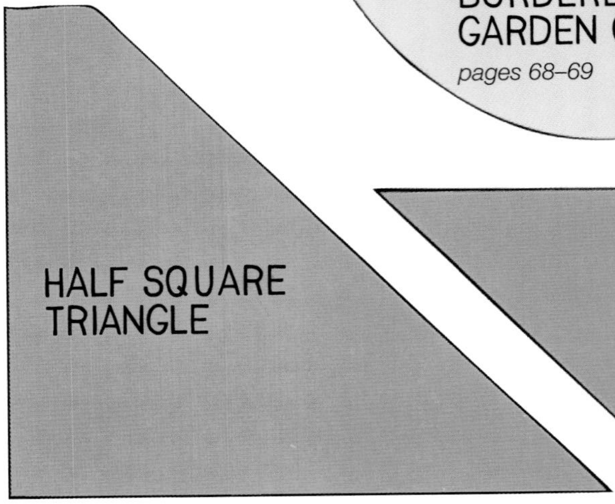

HALF SQUARE
TRIANGLE

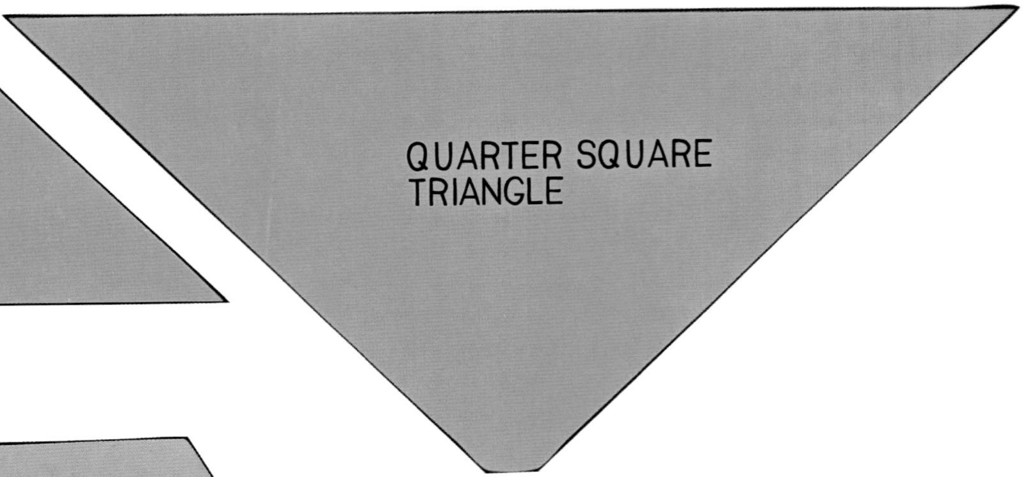

QUARTER SQUARE
TRIANGLE

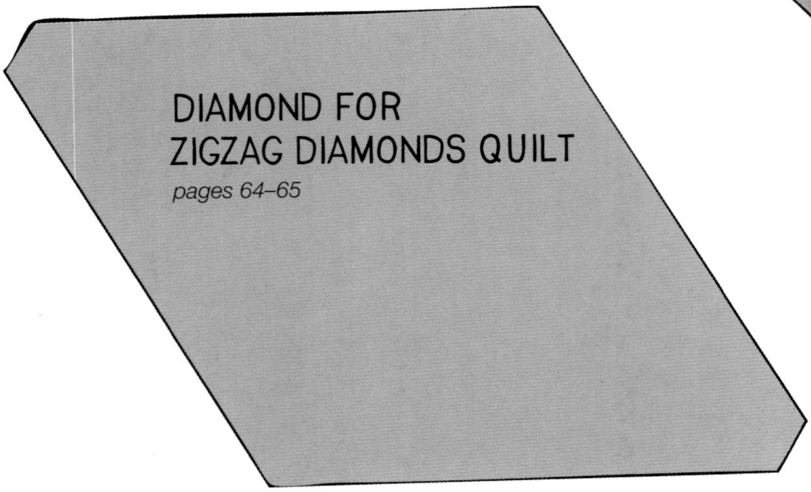

DIAMOND FOR
ZIGZAG DIAMONDS QUILT
pages 64–65

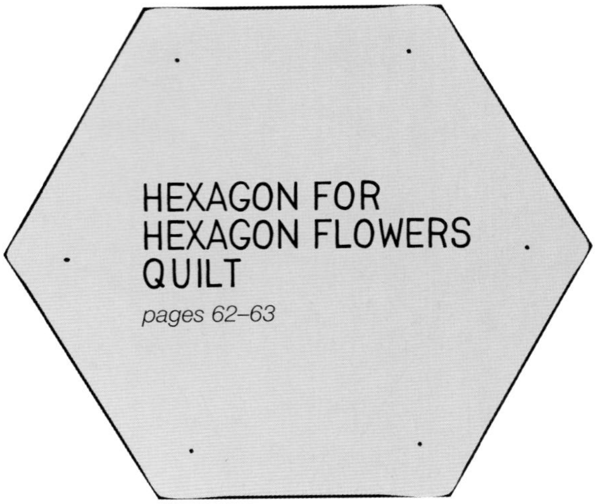

HEXAGON FOR
HEXAGON FLOWERS
QUILT
pages 62–63

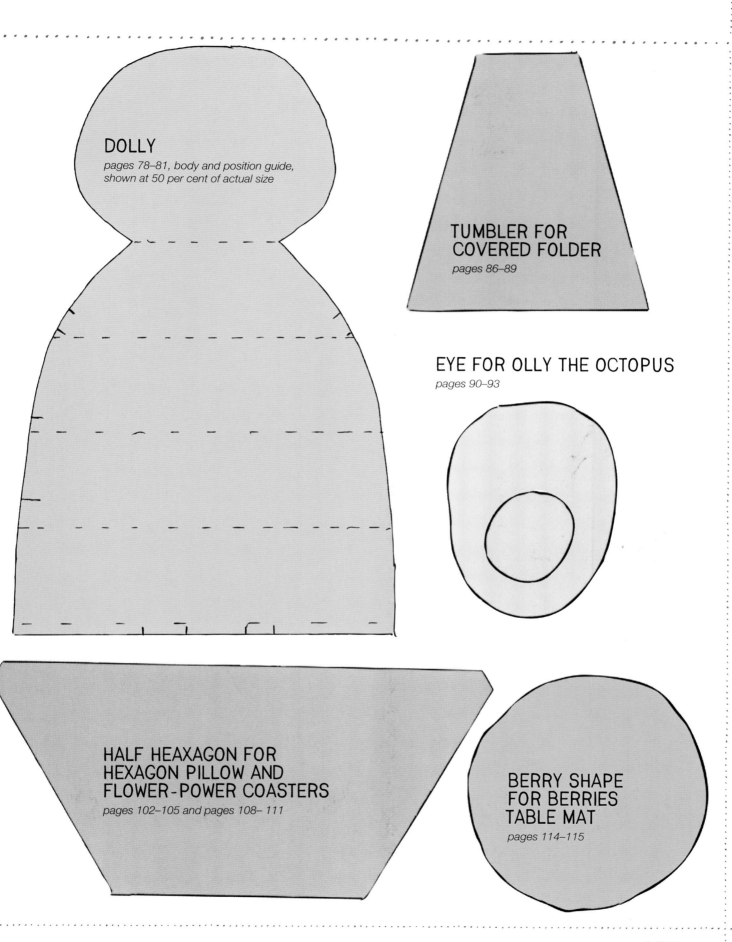

DOLLY
pages 78–81, body and position guide, shown at 50 per cent of actual size

TUMBLER FOR COVERED FOLDER
pages 86–89

EYE FOR OLLY THE OCTOPUS
pages 90–93

HALF HEAXAGON FOR HEXAGON PILLOW AND FLOWER-POWER COASTERS
pages 102–105 and pages 108– 111

BERRY SHAPE FOR BERRIES TABLE MAT
pages 114–115

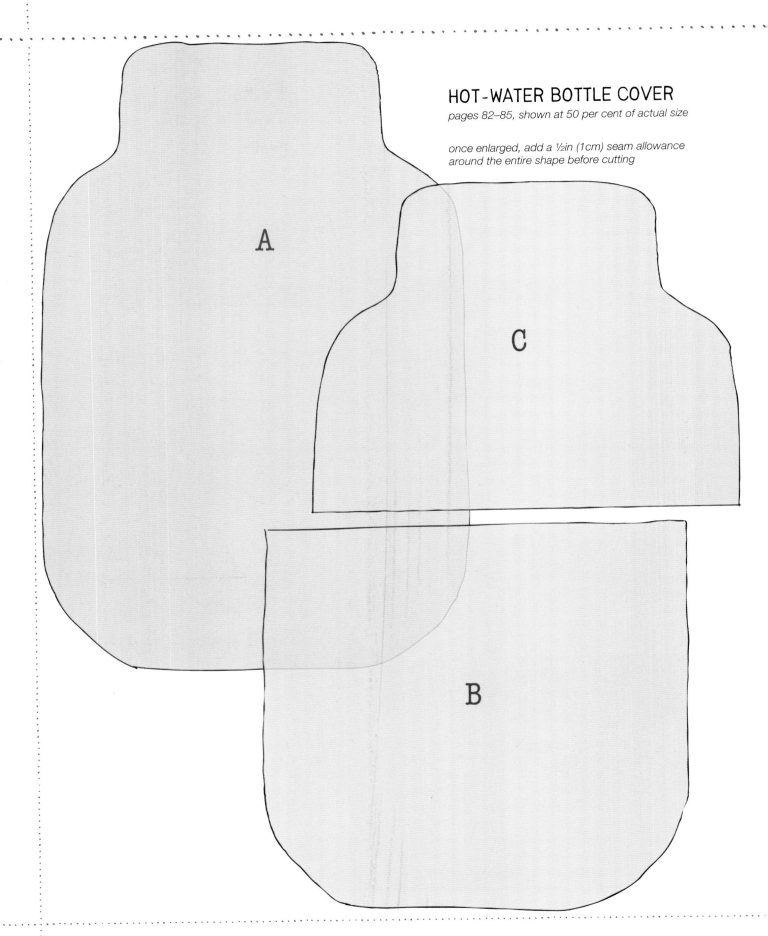

HOT-WATER BOTTLE COVER
pages 82–85, shown at 50 per cent of actual size

once enlarged, add a ½in (1cm) seam allowance around the entire shape before cutting

A

C

B

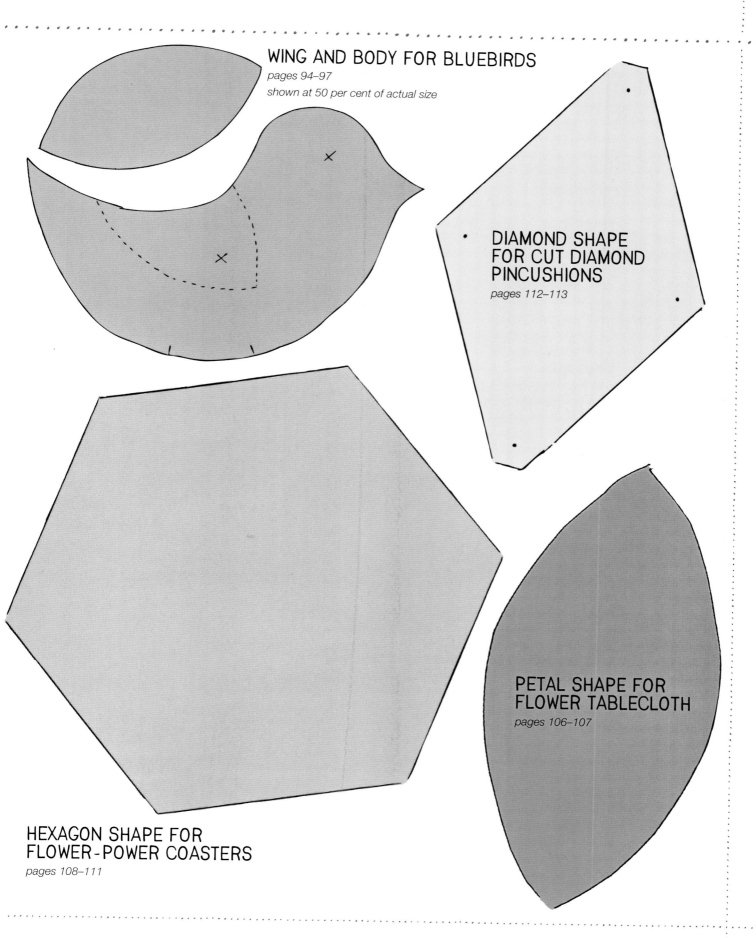

WING AND BODY FOR BLUEBIRDS
pages 94–97
shown at 50 per cent of actual size

DIAMOND SHAPE
FOR CUT DIAMOND
PINCUSHIONS
pages 112–113

PETAL SHAPE FOR
FLOWER TABLECLOTH
pages 106–107

HEXAGON SHAPE FOR
FLOWER-POWER COASTERS
pages 108–111

INDEX